DISCARD

CONCISE
LINCOLN
LIBRARY

—

EDITED BY RICHARD W. ETULAIN,
SARA VAUGHN GABBARD, AND
SYLVIA FRANK RODRIGUE

BRIAN R. DIRCK

Lincoln and the Constitution

Southern Illinois University Press
Carbondale and Edwardsville

The Concise Lincoln Library has been made possible
in part through a generous donation by the Leland E.
and LaRita R. Boren Trust.

Library of Congress Cataloging-in-Publication Data
Dirck, Brian R., 1965–
Lincoln and the Constitution / Brian R. Dirck.
    p. cm. — (Concise Lincoln library)
Includes bibliographical references and index.
ISBN-13: 978-0-8093-3117-8 (cloth : alk. paper)
ISBN-10: 0-8093-3117-9 (cloth : alk. paper)
ISBN-13: 978-0-8093-3118-5 (ebook)
ISBN-10: 0-8093-3118-7 (ebook)
1. Lincoln, Abraham, 1809–1865—Views on the Con-
stitution. 2. Lincoln, Abraham, 1809–1865—Political
and social views. 3. Lincoln, Abraham, 1809–1865—
Views on slavery. 4. United States—Politics and govern-
ment—1783–1865. 5. Constitutional history—United
States. 6. Slaves—Emancipation—United States.
I. Title.
E457.2.D574 2012
973.7092—dc23   2011032610

Printed on recycled paper. ♻
The paper used in this publication meets the minimum
requirements of American National Standard for Information Sciences—Petrmanence of Paper for Printed
Library Materials, ANSI Z39.48-1992. ♾

In memory of Phillip S. Paludan, 1938–2007

CONTENTS

Prologue 1

1 The Constitution in Lincoln's Early Years 6

2 Lincoln, the Constitution, and Slavery
during the Sectional Crisis 17

3 Lincoln and the Declaration of Independence 33

4 Becoming President and Defending the Union 51

5 The War, Civil Liberties, and *Ex Parte Merryman* 68

6 Congress and Winning the War 86

7 Lincoln and the Radicals 99

8 The War and African Americans 115

Epilogue 131

Acknowledgments 139

Notes 141

Bibliography 157

Index 165

Lincoln and the Constitution

PROLOGUE

"That means nigger equality. Now, by God! I'll put him through."[1]

John Wilkes Booth muttered those words to his accomplice, David Herold, as the two men stood in a crowd gathered around the White House on the evening of April 11, 1865. By this time, Booth's thoughts had already turned from kidnapping to assassination. But Lincoln's speech, delivered to the crowd in response to the tidings that Robert E. Lee had surrendered and the Confederate capital city of Richmond, Virginia, was now in Union hands, apparently further hardened Booth's resolve. Lincoln said something in his speech that served to push Booth even further over the edge.

What exactly was the "that" in Lincoln's speech that Booth believed meant "nigger equality," and in his mind provided justification for murder? Lincoln emphasized two broad themes related to American race relations: the need for a constitutional amendment finally and fully outlawing slavery, and the possibility that African American men might be given the vote. Booth's outburst has usually been interpreted as an instance of his venting displeasure at the racial component of Lincoln's speech. The president was directing the country down a radically new path, and Booth was a self-professed Southerner whose bigotry ran deep.[2]

But there was another layer underneath Lincoln's proposals in that last speech. In speaking of the end of slavery and black suffrage, he referenced not only policy decisions, but also potential changes to the US Constitution, in the guise of what would eventually become the Thirteenth and Fifteenth Amendments. Such changes would be permanent. Had Lincoln merely expressed a political or personal preference for a greater degree of what Booth derisively styled "nigger equality," then Booth might have hoped for (what would have seemed to him) better days, when Lincoln and his party could be voted out of office, executive orders canceled, laws passed by Congress changed or superseded. But the Constitution? That carried the unmistakable aura of durability, an aura that may have provided just a bit extra nudge for Booth when he reached for his derringer.

Therein lies a basic truth about the American system. The Constitution and the values surrounding it act as bedrock, a foundational narrative that shapes and guides Americans' political decisions. American constitutionalism is about the first principles, fundamental values, and basic substructure that shape and set the ground rules for our ongoing national political conversation.

The story of Lincoln's personal and political journey towards that day in April 1865, when he became the first sitting president to openly endorse African American suffrage, and by which time he had already sealed his legacy as the Great Emancipator and savior of the Union, has been told many, many times. But the constitutional dimension of this journey? Not quite so much; or rather, not in a way that is immediately available or appealing to a broad reading audience. There are fine scholarly studies focusing specifically on Lincoln's constitutionalism by (among others) George Anastoplo, Daniel Farber, and George P. Fletcher.[3] There are excellent studies of Lincoln's life and career with a good infusion of constitutional analysis, by (again, among others) Phillip Paludan, Mark Neely, and James McPherson.[4] The rather extensive subgenre of scholarly essay collections on Lincoln also offer occasional nuggets of insight into Lincoln's ideas about the Constitution.[5]

So there is actually an extensive collection of books, articles, and monographs on Lincoln's constitutionalism, scattered here and there within the supremely vast field of Lincoln studies. But for all the sophistication and complexity of this literature, we lack something relatively straightforward and basic: an overview of Lincoln's constitutional thought, spanning his entire lifetime. That is the purpose of this book.

The reader should note that this book is aimed primarily at the general reading audience, providing both a readable overview of Lincoln's views on the US Constitution and a starting point for further inquiry. It is not intended to be a comprehensive academic study of the subject, which would be impossible given the purpose and scope of the Concise Lincoln Library series. There are aspects which I have been constrained to treat with brevity—for example, the complex interplay between radical, moderate, and conservative elements in Congress when formulating wartime policymaking—focusing instead on those issues I believe constitute the core of Lincoln's constitutional thought. The book's bibliography provides a solid starting point for those wishing to engage in further investigation.

In writing this account, I have defined "Constitution" broadly, examining not only what Abraham Lincoln said and did about the nation's founding document itself, but also the set of values, assumptions, and judgments that underlie the first principles of his political and intellectual world. In doing so, I have tried to keep forays into the more abstract and technical areas of constitutional theory and law to a minimum. My primary interest is the ongoing interplay in Lincoln's life of his personal goals, his political ideology, and his constitutional thought.

As we will see, Lincoln's constitutionalism did have certain basic, consistent characteristics: foundational principles that were, on the whole, quite well thought out and carefully reasoned. That said, however, it is important to remember that Lincoln was not an intellectual, formulating his ideas in a vacuum of abstraction. He was a practical man and a pragmatic politician, often forced by the ever-changing circumstances of his remarkably volatile time to formulate solutions to problems on the fly, with few reliable guidelines or precedents. American constitutionalism during the Civil War was filled with blind spots and unforeseen eventualities. Readers will note how often a discussion of a given aspect of the Constitution began with some variation of "no one really knew." Lincoln found himself filling these blank spaces in the American constitutional tradition, particularly while he occupied the White House.

There have been those who see this filling of constitutional blank spaces as an act of repairing a severely flawed instrument. Justice Thurgood Marshall, for example, during the bicentennial of the Constitution in 1987, argued that the Founding Fathers had created at best an imperfect union two hundred years previously, one shot through with shortsighted and morally dubious compromises, particularly where race and slavery were concerned. "I do not believe that the meaning of the Constitution was forever 'fixed' at the Philadelphia Convention," Marshall declared. "Nor do I find the wisdom, foresight, and sense of justice exhibited by the Framers particularly profound. To the contrary, the government they devised was defective from the start, requiring several amendments, a civil war, and momentous social transformation to attain the system of constitutional government, and its respect for the individual freedoms and human rights, we hold as fundamental today."[6]

There is truth to Justice Marshall's argument, and I think Lincoln would have sympathized with his point of view, at least where race and slavery entered the conversation. "Your race are suffering, in my judgment, the greatest wrong inflicted on any people," Lincoln told a group of African Americans who met with him during the war. Before the war he, was deeply troubled by the Constitution's various compromises with slavery. "I also acknowledge *your* rights and *my* obligations, under the constitution, in regard to your slaves," he wrote to a Southern friend in 1855. "I confess I hate to see the poor creatures hunted down, and caught, and carried back to their stripes, and unrewarded toils; but I bite my lip and keep quiet."[7]

Still, Lincoln saw the Constitution of 1787 as a fixed instrument, "the pivotal event in our national history, the event that constituted our national identity," to quote historian Hendrik Hartog. For Lincoln, there were certain timeless principles—the rule of law, the efficacy and wisdom of democracy, the basic liberty endowed to all citizens—embodied in the Constitution that did not and should not be changed. They were principles put there by man, in the name of God.[8]

Lincoln took an essentially optimistic view of the Constitution, in both its structure as he found it, and its potential to effect positive change in the American future. If there is an overriding theme to Lincoln's relationship with the US Constitution, it is this never fully extinguished faith that the nation's founding document, and the values it represented, were vehicles for advancing that which was good and just.

In some ways it is quite striking: This often morose, fatalistic man, awash in a sea of controversy and blood, somehow managed to keep faith that the Constitution he admired and swore to protect was equal to the severe trials of the age.

THE CONSTITUTION IN
LINCOLN'S EARLY YEARS

Born into a hardscrabble life on the fringes of polite American society in 1809, Abraham Lincoln was not groomed to think high thoughts about the US Constitution, or much of anything else. The semiliterate farmers around him equated reading, other than the Bible or *Pilgrim's Progress*, with idleness—wasted time that was better spent on the business end of a plow or axe. "Abe was awful lazy," recalled one of his Indiana neighbors; "he worked for me . . . a few days only at a time. [He] was always reading and thinking [and I] used to get mad at him."[1]

His first exposure to the Constitution, such as it was, probably came in one of the early biographies he read of George Washington when he was a boy, or perhaps in other accounts he might have read of the Founding Fathers and the Revolutionary era.[2] It wouldn't have been much, this early exposure to the Constitution—like any other young boy his age, he would have surely been far more interested in stories about Revolutionary War battles and the romantic rendering of the Founders' heroic wartime exploits common to the histories of the age. But this literature would at least have linked the nation's founding document to the Revolutionary generation and Lincoln's most revered heroes, like George Washington. "Washington is the mightiest name of earth," he declared years later in a speech on Washington's birthday; "on that name, an eulogy is expected. It cannot be. To add brightness to the sun, or glory to the name of Washington, is alike impossible. Let none attempt it."[3]

Lincoln's reverence for Washington and his generation would have connected the Constitution with things sacred, and a new, powerful American civic religion of reverence for the Revolutionary generation and its seminal works. Lincoln was a true believer. "Let every American, every lover of liberty, every well wisher to his posterity, swear by the blood of the Revolution, never to violate in the least particular, the laws of the country; and never to tolerate their violation by others," he exhorted in one of his earliest speeches. "As the patriots of seventy-six did to the support of the Declaration of Independence, so to the support of the Constitution and Laws, let every American pledge his life, his property, and his sacred honor."[4]

In this, Lincoln was not terribly unique. Many Americans of his time harbored a quasi-mystical nationalism that combined secular religious symbolism and pageantry—Fourth of July celebrations, for example—what modern generations might describe as a "cult of personality" centered primarily on George Washington, and a deep-seated reverence for the hallowed texts of the Revolutionary generation, of which the 1787 Constitution was the most conspicuous.[5]

Lincoln's early years afforded him few opportunities to encounter the Constitution in any other more systematic manner. Striking out on his own at age twenty-two, Lincoln drifted into the little river village of New Salem, Illinois, and there spent several years as a local jack-of-all-trades: general store clerk, land surveyor, postmaster (at "a very small office"), flatboat crewman, and farm laborer when absolutely necessary. "This procured bread, and kept soul and body together," he later wrote.[6]

While living in New Salem, he sometimes watched the proceedings in the local town court and occasionally participated as an impromptu advocate, there being no actual lawyers in the tiny town. He undertook study for the bar in earnest during the early 1830s, during which time he likely first read and studied the entire text of the Constitution. But this would have been a relatively secondary concern, as he would have been far more preoccupied with learning the intricacies of the law's everyday machinery.[7]

His basic legal textbook was Sir William Blackstone's *Commentaries on the Laws of England*, the all-important treatise on the English legal system that served as a portal into the law for generations of American lawyers.[8] Blackstone would have said nothing at all about the American Constitution, of course; the first edition was written in 1765, and it focused on the English common-law system. But the *Commentaries* did give Lincoln an appreciation for the rule of law, and an understanding of its basic framework and rationale—for constitutionalism, if not necessarily the Constitution. Blackstone encouraged his readers to think of the law as an elegant structure of logic and reason, the best human beings had to offer in the way of understanding justice and conflict resolution in a community, stripped of superfluities and errors by the engine of reason, and yet also anchored in the wisdom of the past. Blackstone fairly gushed in his admiration for the British constitutional system, "perhaps the only one in the universe, in which political or civil liberty, is the very end and scope."[9]

If the various Washington biographies Lincoln read gave his constitutionalism a romanticized tint, then Blackstone helped give it a conservative streak, if by "conservative" we mean a respect for past tradition, and a tendency to give lawmakers—whether they be, in Blackstone's case, English jurists, or, in Lincoln's case, the Framers of the Constitution—the benefit of the doubt. When Blackstone referenced the "constitution," he did so with the English model in mind, a model that defined "constitution" as the corpus of laws and customs that constituted the English common-law system, rather than a specific written charter like the US Constitution. Relatively few legal treatises dealing directly with the American document were available to law student Lincoln. Joseph Story published his *Commentaries on the Constitution of the United States* in 1833, at the very time Lincoln was trying to master Blackstone, but it is unlikely that Lincoln was able to procure a copy of such a relatively new text on the Illinois frontier.

After passing his bar exam in 1836, he went about the business of building a practice, relocating to the bustling new town of Springfield, and plying his wares in courthouses up and down central Illinois's Eighth Judicial Circuit. For twenty-five years, he litigated every type of case for every type of client, very few of which concerned either the US Constitution or constitutional issues in general.

But even if he did not often directly encounter the Constitution in the courtroom, Lincoln's law practice was nevertheless another important brick in the foundation of his constitutionalism. Constitutionalism is, among other things, a sense of how the law should function. Lincoln's practice gave him an understanding of the various ways that the law worked itself out in the everyday lives of ordinary Americans, experiences that in turn gave him a deep pragmatic streak, as well as an appreciation for legal arguments that were simple and straightforward and avoided flamboyance. "In law it is good policy to never *plead* what you *need* not, lest you oblige yourself to *prove* what you *can* not," he admonished.[10]

Throughout his life, whenever Lincoln encountered thorny problems, his lawyerly instincts told him to value workable solutions, avoid showdowns, and exercise whenever possible the art of compromise. "Discourage litigation," he advised fellow attorneys. "Persuade your neighbors to compromise whenever you can. Point out to them how the nominal winner is often a real loser—in fees, expenses, and waste of time. As a peacemaker the lawyer has a superior opportunity of being a good man. There will still be business enough." It was a philosophy that he would apply time and again throughout not only his legal career, but his political career, as well.[11]

Lincoln had a little more to say directly about the Constitution in the political realm—but not much, at least early on. All politics are local, after all, and Lincoln's early speeches during his campaigns for the Illinois legislature (he lost in 1832 but won the first of his four terms two years later) stressed issues of interest to Illinois voters.[12]

Unlike his Illinois farming neighbors, who were usually Jacksonian Democrats, Lincoln joined the Whig Party, which possessed roots stretching back to the old Federalist Party of the Founding era, the party of Alexander Hamilton, and a strong national government. For Hamiltonian Federalists, a strong national government was necessary for good business, and the Constitution should be interpreted accordingly. Federalists supported a school of thought known as "broad constructionism"—meaning interpretation of the

Constitution's language giving the broadest possible latitude to the words and the powers they invest in the national government. "There are implied as well as expressed powers" in the Constitution, Hamilton wrote. "The only question must be . . . whether the means to be employed . . . [have] a natural relation to any of the acknowledged objects or lawful ends of the government."[13]

Hamilton's political opponent Thomas Jefferson, and his party, the Jeffersonian-Republicans, countered with what came to be known as a "strict constructionist" approach to the Constitution—that is, limiting the national government to only those powers explicitly mentioned in the document. "I consider the foundation of the Constitution as laid on this ground, that 'all powers not delegated to the United States, by the Constitution, nor prohibited by it to the States, are reserved to the States or to the people.'" Jefferson wrote. "To take a single step beyond the boundaries thus specially drawn around the powers of Congress, is to take possession of a boundless field of power, no longer susceptible of any definition," and therefore liable to the creation of a national government grounded in tyranny.[14]

Lincoln was very much a Hamiltonian, broad constructionist in his interpretation of the US Constitution. He saw the Constitution less as a limiter on national government action, and more as a catalyst for necessary economic development. He had little patience with Jeffersonian Democrats' assertion that the Founding Fathers held such a limited view of federal authority. "The Constitution enumerates expressly several powers which Congress may exercise, superadded to which is a general authority 'to make all laws necessary and proper,' for carrying into effect all the powers vested by the Constitution of the Government of the United States," he pointed out in an early speech on the power of the national government to charter a national bank. That rather vague language, "necessary and proper," was plenty good enough, as far as Lincoln was concerned. "One of the express powers given Congress, is 'To lay and collect taxes; duties, imposts, and excises; to pay the debts, and provide for the common defence [*sic*] and general welfare of the United States.' Now, Congress is expressly authorized to make all laws necessary and proper for carrying this power into execution. To carry it into execution, it is indispensably necessary to collect, safely keep, transfer, and disburse a revenue. To do this, a Bank is 'necessary and proper.'"[15]

On a personal level, Lincoln liked and admired ambitious entrepreneurs of the sort who welcomed cooperation between government and business in the name of economic development. He valued manual laborers and farmers (though he was not especially interested in such pursuits for his own career choice), but he wanted government and popular support for commerce, banking, and other capitalist interests. "That men who are industrious, and sober, and honest in the pursuit of their own interests should after a while accumulate capital, and after that should be allowed to enjoy it in peace, and also if they should choose when they have accumulated it to use it to save themselves from actual labor and hire other people to labor for them is right," he declared. And he wanted the system—legal, constitutional, and political—to actively support such pursuits.[16]

His Constitution was a vigorous, flexible instrument, with the latent power in its language necessary to allow the government room to grow and maneuver, and to meet the exigencies of new times and challenges. Lincoln wanted a Constitution with teeth. This did not mean, however, that he advocated a dangerous, runaway interpretation of the Constitution that might justify any sort of power grab by the national government and its leaders. He was always sensitive to the possibility of tyranny and usurpation of power by ambitious American politicians. "Many great and good men sufficiently qualified for any task they should undertake, may ever be found, whose ambition would aspire to nothing beyond a seat in Congress, a gubernatorial or a presidential chair," he pointed out in his speech at the Springfield Lyceum; "*but such belong not to the family of the lion, or the tribe of the eagle*[.] What! think you these places would satisfy an Alexander, a Caesar, or a Napoleon? Never! Towering genius disdains a beaten path. . . . Is it unreasonable then to expect, that some man possessed of the loftiest genius, coupled with ambition sufficient to push it to its utmost stretch, will at some time, spring up among us? And when such a one does, it will require the people to be united with each other, attached to the government and laws, and generally intelligent, to successfully frustrate his designs."[17]

Taken altogether, Lincoln's early constitutionalism was a balancing act, one that definitely leaned towards the Hamiltonian model of broad constructionism and a robust rendering of national power, but at the same time respected the rule of law and the limitations placed by the Constitution's legal and political system on people's actions. Lincoln wanted an energetic but not a dangerous government, and he wanted a flexible but not infinitely malleable Constitution. Beneath it all he wanted a visceral connection between Americans and their government institutions, a reverence for the spirit of 1787 and the works of the Founding Fathers, with shades of Parson Weems and his romanticized vision of George Washington and the American Revolution.

None of these aspects of Lincoln's constitutionalism had much to do with slavery—at least prior to 1854.

Lincoln hated slavery. Even before the Civil War and his eventual role as the Great Emancipator, his speeches and letters were littered with tart references to the peculiar institution: "All agreed that slavery was an evil"; "the most dumb and stupid slave that ever toiled for a master, does constantly *know* that he is wronged"; "although volume upon volume is written to prove slavery a very good thing, we never hear of the man who wishes to take the good of it, *by being a slave himself*"; "If A. can prove, however conclusively, that he may, of right, enslave B.—why may not B. snatch the same argument, and prove equally, that he may enslave A?" "I have always hated slavery, as much I think as any abolitionist," he claimed. This was true.[18]

"The slavery question often bothered me as far back as 1836–1840," he later claimed.[19] This was probably true, as far as it went. But while slavery did bother him, it did not preoccupy him. Other matters dominated his attention and his politics. Before 1854, he talked more often about economics and the Whig Party's system of government-sponsored release of American business energy than he did about human bondage. Slavery and its attendant concerns only rarely popped to the surface.

When they did so, Lincoln was a consistent, principled but cautious critic. His first recorded political stance against slavery came in 1837. That year he cosponsored an antislavery petition in the Illinois legislature, claiming that the institution "is founded on both injustice and bad policy." The petition also argued that Congress possessed the power to abolish slavery in the District of Columbia.[20] This was a cause near and dear to many abolitionists' hearts.

The federal government's constitutional authority over slavery in the individual states was open to debate, and a matter of heated controversy. One school of thought among radical antislavery activists called for immediate, unambiguous federal action to ban slavery entirely, and they developed controversial arguments to support their cause. They believed that the Founding Fathers were demonstrably antislavery at heart, because of their refusal to use the word "slavery" directly in the Constitution (preferring instead euphemisms such as "persons held to involuntary servitude"), and because they banned slavery from the Northwest Territory (the future states of Ohio, Illinois, Indiana, Michigan and Wisconsin) in 1787.[21]

Moreover, "natural law," which radical antislavery writers defined as an element of constitutionalism rooted in universal principles of justice, mitigated against the American legal system as giving slavery anything more than at best temporary protection. "If the majority, however large, of the people of a country, enter into a contract of government, called a constitution, be which they agree to aid, abet or accomplish any kind of injustice [that is, slavery] . . . this contract is unlawful and void," claimed antislavery constitutionalist Lysander Spooner. By this thinking, the nation's Constitution, rooted as it was in the same natural law of the Declaration of Independence and the principles of the Revolution, must be invoked, sooner or later, to end the injustice of human bondage.[22]

But the vast majority of Americans—even those who didn't like slavery—weren't so sure. Allow Washington to reach directly into the slaveholding states and interfere with a system of labor that touched upon the daily lives of millions of Americans, black and white, despite state laws and regulations to the contrary? Not many people were inclined to begin the slide down that slippery slope. If the federal government could thus run roughshod over white Southern sensibilities, where would it end? The national government would in effect be the arbiter of its own authority, unchecked by average citizens or the language of the Constitution. "The principle and construction . . . that the general government is the exclusive judge of the extent of the powers delegated to it, stop nothing short of despotism," argued Thomas Jefferson in the Kentucky Resolution of 1799, "since the discretion of those who administer the government, and not the constitution, would be the measure of their powers."[23]

Even those people not otherwise inclined to agree with Jefferson on most matters were generally in agreement on this subject. While there were plenty of nationalistic Americans—supporters of Alexander Hamilton and his Federalist Party in the early decades of the nation's existence, and later the Whigs—even the most fervent believers in a strong federal regime nevertheless felt the day-to-day functions of governing America must remain in local hands. Americans consequently saw to it that the federal government had almost no direct presence in their lives.[24]

Before Americans engaged the question of how whites should treat blacks on a moral level, they needed to first address the constitutional issue of which branch of government—if any—could tell them how to behave at all. Abolitionists' demands for top-down action from Washington, DC, subsequently met almost insuperable resistance from ordinary Americans prior to the even dicier and emotional racial dimensions of slavery and race. A modern American might see in proposals for federal antislavery intervention an admirable attempt to use the long arm of federal law to protect African Americans, and there would be truth in this. But white Americans of Lincoln's time saw something else entirely; not a protective arm but rather a clenched fist, poised to create Jefferson's tyranny.

The antislavery petition Lincoln signed was written in direct response to a report from a legislative subcommittee that held that, while slavery offered the repugnant spectacle of an "unfortunate condition of our fellow men, whose lots are cast in thraldom [sic] in a land of liberty and peace," nevertheless "the arm of the general Government has no power to strike their fetters from them."[25] This was typically where the national debate concerning slavery began and ended—arguments over the federal government's constitutional power vis-à-vis the states, while the actual moral problems associated with human bondage were shunted to one side.

But the District of Columbia was another matter entirely. Congress's authority over the nation's capital was incontrovertible. Article I, Section 8 of the Constitution made Congress the legislative governing body for the district. It therefore possessed the legal power to abolish the trafficking in human beings that occurred on the streets of Washington. "We consider it as a grievance that citizens . . . should be permitted to come into the district, and pursue a traffic fraught with so much misery to a class of beings entitled to our protection, by the laws of justice and humanity," wrote one outraged abolitionist.[26]

Abolitionists saw the question of slavery in Washington, DC, as a small but vital first step towards the eventual national eradication of the institution, because it did not instantly devolve into yet another interminable states' rights vs. federal government debate. Most Americans conceded that Congress could act against slavery in Washington, if it chose to do so. Even white Southerners were inclined to acquiesce on this matter, albeit reluctantly, and claiming all the while that congressional action against slavery in the district without some sort of referendum would constitute a breach of faith with the district's citizens.[27]

If antislavery Americans persuaded Congress to move—perhaps by first abolishing the city's slave trade, and then banning slavery entirely—they might set a political and moral precedent for the rest of the country. "This trade in blood; this buying, imprisoning, and exporting of boys and girls eight years old; this tearing asunder of husbands and wives, parents and children, is all legalized in virtue of authority delegated by congress!" read one furious abolitionist broadside—and presumably congressional action to end these practices would set a laudable example.[28]

Lincoln agreed that Congress ought to take some action against the slave trafficking that occurred practically in its own front yard. But his embrace of the cause for freedom in the nation's capital was qualified. While acknowledging that Congress could act to abolish DC's slave trafficking whenever it chose to do so, the petition echoed the desires of white Southerners when it cautioned "that that power ought not to be exercised unless at the request of the people of said District." Moreover, the petition distanced its supporters from abolitionism, declaring that "the promulgation of abolitionist doctrines tends rather to increase than to abate [slavery's] evils."[29]

Lincoln's faith in the American political system ran deeper than that of many radical abolitionists, and he showed little sympathy with Americans who risked wrecking the nation's constitutional system in the name of abolitionism. "Those who would shiver into fragments the Union of these States; tear to tatters its now venerated constitution; and even burn the last copy of the Bible, rather than slavery should continue a single hour, together with all their more halting sympathisers, have received, and are receiving their just execration," he believed.[30] His perspective on reformers generally was that of guarded respect, but he felt meaningful change must happen slowly, carefully, and within the machinery of the political system. He did not believe that the law could be used to enact sudden, radical social change. It could not soften the hardened hearts of American racists, and it could not make possible what he thought to be impossible—a peaceful level of social and political equality between black and white people.

Lincoln's overall approach to slavery and race during the early years of his political career was generally hazy. He was on the more enlightened—if not perfect—side of white opinion where everyday relations with individual people of color were concerned. He was a convinced and consistent critic of slavery, and he showed real political courage in embracing any antislavery petitions on the floor of the Illinois legislature, even a petition as limited as the 1837 document. Many a white politician in his day hesitated to do even this, lest he be labeled an abolitionist or worse, which was political suicide in the hothouse racial climate of the day.

But the Abraham Lincoln of the 1840s and early 1850s had not put much effort or energy into developing a coherent antislavery ideology. Nor would he press his antislavery convictions to the point of a radical antislavery reading of the Constitution. Or at least, he would not do before 1854.

LINCOLN, THE CONSTITUTION,
AND SLAVERY DURING THE
SECTIONAL CRISIS

In 1854, Lincoln emerged out of a semiretirement from politics and reentered the fray, armed with a powerful, morally righteous anger against slavery, and equally powerful constitutional arguments to combat the institution and hopefully set it, as he put it, "in [the] course of ultimate extinction."[1]

In May of that year, Congress passed the Kansas-Nebraska Act, marking a major turning point for the United States in its ongoing sectional crisis between North and South. Controversial from its very inception, the act was "more celebrated (for the censure by its enemies, and praise by its friends) than any act of Congress since the foundation of the government," according to one contemporary observer. Even its author, Stephen Douglas, acknowledged that Kansas-Nebraska was bound to create "a hell of a storm."[2]

The storm came because the Kansas-Nebraska Act profoundly changed the way Americans dealt with the thorny matter of what to do about slavery's future expansion into the western territories. It was thorny because slavery's expansion westward was by definition a national problem. Most other slavery-related issues were not. Slaves were held in bondage by a complicated web of local rules, regulations, and customs. The Constitution did involve the federal government in slavery, it is true, but concerning largely peripheral matters like the international slave trade (banned by the Constitution after 1808, and a relatively minor problem thereafter), and the Article IV provision requiring free states to return runaway slaves.

These provisions were important in that they gave slavery the imprimatur of national approval and morally tainted the nation's founding document. But in practical terms, the Constitution only minimally impacted the day-to-day operations of the slave system. Add to this the absence of any nationwide media—really few national institutions of any kind—and it is little wonder that slavery was conceptualized by most Americans as a local institution. As long as this was so, Northerners could convince themselves that slavery was none of their business: out of sight, out of mind.

But this approach did not work where slavery and western expansion were concerned. Article IV, Section 3 of the Constitution put Congress squarely in charge of new territories, empowering the nation's legislature to "dispose of and make all needful Rules and Regulations respecting the Territory or other Property belonging to the United States." This solved the problem of states fighting with one another over new western lands, but it also meant that Americans were now required by their own Constitution to perennially engage in a national conversation about slavery whenever the nation added new territory. They could talk about almost any other issue, and while they sometimes shouted at one another, they still talked. Slavery, on the other hand, moved people to shout, wave fists, threaten violence, and perhaps even end the conversation entirely.

The issue actually predated the Constitution itself. In 1787—while the states were still united under the old Articles of Confederation—Congress passed the Northwest Ordinance. A blueprint for settling the new western territories located in and around the Great Lakes region, the ordinance declared. "There shall be neither slavery nor involuntary servitude in the said territory, otherwise than in the punishment of crimes whereof the party shall have been duly convicted." Antislavery Americans—including Lincoln—would later use the Northwest Ordinance as proof that the Founding Fathers did not want slavery to spread into new western lands.[3]

In 1803, President Jefferson bought from France what would become the middle third of the United States. Now Americans possessed many thousands of miles of western territory that had no immediately discernible future where slavery was concerned; and predictably enough, the situation rapidly escalated into a full-blown crisis. Southern slaveholders demanded a slice of the new western pie, while Northerners denied that human bondage could or should be introduced into the West. "Doubtless it is the duty of Congress . . . to incorporate into the union parts of the territory beyond the Mississippi, at such periods, and on such terms, as a regard to the general good shall dictate," argued an antislavery Northerner; and "if the general good requires that slavery shall be forever excluded from the new states, then Congress is bound to exclude it." By 1820, these arguments had grown heated enough that they threatened to engulf the nation in a civil war.[4]

Into the maelstrom of controversy stepped Lincoln's hero, Henry Clay. Then a promising young congressman from Kentucky, Clay brokered a compromise that drew a line across the middle of the Louisiana Purchase at the 36°30' parallel, north of which slavery would be prohibited (save for the state of Missouri itself, already established as slave territory north of that line), and south of which slavery would be permitted. The nation breathed a collective sigh of relief. "Thank God, it is, at last, decided; and, as we believe, decided right," wrote the editor of the Baltimore *Patriot*.[5]

The compromise's meaning was open to different interpretations. Southerners saw it as a guarantee that their way of life had a future. They were convinced that slavery must expand to survive, and the compromise line allowed the institution to do so, in Missouri and in what would eventually become the slave states of Arkansas and Louisiana.[6] But for antislavery Northerners like Lincoln, the compromise line was not a guardian; it was a quarantine line stretched across the western territories, designed to contain the crime scene of slavery. Once hemmed in, slavery could eventually die a natural death.[7]

But Free-Soil Northerners greatly overestimated the extent to which white Southerners might be willing to part with slavery under any circumstances. They also underestimated the nearly intractable social, cultural, and political problems emancipation faced in the South, even with emancipation plans that pushed the slaves' eventual freedom decades into the hazy future. Perhaps most of all, they underestimated the ambition and political skills of Illinois senator and presidential aspirant Stephen Douglas.

Douglas, the so-called "little steam engine in britches," was a consummate political manipulator, perhaps the best of his age, deftly maneuvering allies and foes alike to get what he wanted. He had little patience with dreamers of any stripe, and he was above all a political horse trader who would deal with whomever he had to, to get what he needed. "The propulsive force of an idea in his own mind depended wholly upon its appeal to his practical judgment," wrote one early biographer. "His was the philosophy of the attainable."[8]

But there was more to Stephen Douglas than avarice; a consistent political and constitutional ideology drove his actions. He genuinely believed in the power of democracy. Something of a rags-to-riches story himself, he felt that America's genius lay in its ability to harness the power of the people. His constitutionalism was subsequently a populist reading of the document as empowering the federal government to do whatever was best for ordinary Americans, particularly the white American small farmers who were the backbone of the nation's economy (not to mention his most powerful constituents). He did not much care for the arguments swirling around a strict vs. broad interpretation of constitutional language, and he had little patience with those who wanted to use the Constitution to empower an abstract moral reform movement like abolitionism. The only abstract principle that mattered to him was (white) democracy.[9]

These ideas squared with his political ambitions and his style. A short little man, Douglas was nevertheless a dynamo on the stump, with an uncommonly large head and an uncommonly loud voice (no small matter in the days before microphones) and a combative, irascible disposition that angered his political enemies but endeared him to frontier audiences. "His face was convulsed, his gesticulation frantic, and he lashed himself into such a heat that if his body had been made of combustible matter it would have burnt out," John Quincy Adams sourly noted after witnessing one of Douglas's speeches. "In the midst of his roaring, to save himself from choking, he stripped off and cast away his cravat, unbuttoned his waistcoat, and had the air and aspect of a half-naked pugilist." Adams was disgusted at the spectacle; the rough farmers whose votes Douglas courted were not.[10]

In 1850, Douglas was called upon to harness his passion and political skills regarding another crisis concerning slavery and the West. This time Americans faced the question of what to do about slavery in the territories acquired during the Mexican War—the western portion of the United States. Southerners again demanded a share of the war's western spoils, and Northerners again insisted that slavery had no place in the West. Again the nation was convulsed with dark threats of disunion and civil war.

And again, for one last time, Henry Clay was called upon to broker some sort of compromise. Now a frail seventy-three years old, one of the Senate's lions in winter (he would be dead in two years), Clay negotiated the Compromise of 1850, which fashioned a complicated, careful balance between Northern and Southern interests, the centerpiece of which was extension of the Missouri Compromise line across the West.[11]

Northerners breathed another sigh of relief. President Millard Fillmore praised the compromise as a "final and irrevocable . . . settlement," and Douglas rejoiced that the nation could now "stop the debate, and drop the subject."[12] But white Southerners were uneasy with the compromise. They acquiesced in the measure, but it seemed to many Southerners that the line gave too much territory and power to Northerners, at the South's expense. The compromises of 1820 and 1850 together surrendered a vast, rich region north of the thirty-sixth parallel, Jefferson Davis pointed out, and the North, "having obtained, by those successive cessions, a majority in both houses of Congress, took to itself all the territory acquired by Mexico. Thus, by the action of the general government, the means were provided permanently to destroy the original equilibrium between the sections." That line drawn across the 36°30' parallel truly was beginning to look uncomfortably like a quarantine.[13]

The Compromise of 1850 was closely associated with Henry Clay, but Douglas deserved much of the credit for the measure's success. His various maneuvers ultimately steered the compromise measures through Congress, and his supporters believed the statesmanship and political skills Douglas displayed in securing final passage of the measure made him presidential timber. The Little Giant was now "in the foremost rank among the leading minds of the nation," according to one ally.[14]

Douglas needed Southerners if he was to gain the big prize: the Democratic Party nomination in 1856, and ultimately the White House. No Democrat could hope to win the party's highest honor without Southern support. This need, along with his principled love of American democracy, led Douglas to embrace an idea that had been kicked about in Democratic Party circles for years: popular sovereignty.

Popular sovereignty was a deceptively simple idea, one that appealed to the most basic democratic instincts of the American tradition: Rather than draw a geographic line, let the inhabitants of each territory vote on whether or not they wanted slavery. The constitutional mechanism was likewise straightforward. Congress could exercise its Article IV power to make the rules for each new territory, and under that provision it possessed legal authority to set the rules regarding how a given territory might become a state. No one seriously disputed Congress's power to do so, and no one could, it was thought, assail the wisdom of allowing the people to decide for themselves what they wanted. "Leave to the people who will be affected . . . to adjust [the slavery question] upon their own responsibility and in their own manner," argued Lewis Cass, a Democratic congressman from Michigan, who first proposed the idea when he ran for the presidency in 1848.[15]

Cass's doctrine solved a variety of problems for Douglas. He could propose it to Southerners as an alternative to the Missouri Compromise line, erasing that line in favor of giving them at least a theoretical opportunity to carry their slaves anywhere in the West and creating new slave states, provided they had enough votes to do so. Southerners would be so grateful for the opportunity that they would surely support the Little Giant's bid for the presidency in 1856.

More generally, popular sovereignty was an enticing proposition for many Northerners. Weary of the long fight over slavery in the territories, and suspicious that the Missouri Compromise line would not prove effective in containing slaveholders' interests, many

Northerners thought that Douglas's solution was an ideal way to finally and forever put the matter to rest. Let the nation compete for slavery at the polls. Why not? It seemed an appropriately American-style solution, combining the democratic process with respect for the rights of citizens to determine their own local institutions, with little interference from busybodies in other parts of the nation—abolitionists, for example—trying to tell them how to live their lives. "The people in Kansas and Nebraska have the right, under the Constitution, to determine for themselves any questions affecting their domestic relations, the same as they have in Connecticut or Ohio," declared Democratic congressman and popular sovereignty supporter Charles Ingersoll.[16]

A substantial portion of American opinion held popular sovereignty to be an ideal solution to slavery. Southerners thought it gave them a decent shot at expanding slavery throughout the West. Northerners thought it could get slavery back to the state and local level where it belonged. Stephen Douglas thought it could make him president.

Still, if plenty of Northerners thought popular sovereignty was a capital idea, many others were considerably less enthusiastic. Nowhere was this truer than in the office of Lincoln and Herndon, attorneys-at-law, in downtown Springfield, Illinois.

Stretched out on a worn office sofa that could barely accommodate his six-foot-four-inch frame, Lincoln voraciously read newspapers and kept up with current events, even as he remained largely retired from political life. His brief term in the US Congress had not gone well. He had cut a deal with two other Whigs whereby they would rotate the congressional office representing one of the few safe Whig districts in the state, but towards the end of his term, Lincoln quietly signaled his desire to serve another term. His party did not take him up on the offer. Unable to secure renomination, he returned home to Springfield and found himself largely shut out of the Whig Party's upper circles of influence, even though he campaigned hard for Whig candidate Zachary Taylor.[17] So he went back to his law practice and his growing family and, for a while, was content to let his ambition temporarily cool. "I was losing interest in politics, when the repeal of the Missouri Compromise aroused me again," he later wrote.[18]

"Aroused" appears to have been something of an understatement. Herndon's partner was galvanized by the news that Douglas's bill would open the possibility of slavery's legality in all the western territories. "Now . . . a live issue was presented to him," Herndon wrote. "In the office discussions he grew bolder in his utterances. He insisted that the social and political difference between slavery and freedom was becoming more marked; that one must overcome the other; and that postponing the struggle between them would only make it more deadly in the end." Lincoln himself dramatically described the effect as something as akin to a call to arms for antislavery Northerners. Douglas "took us by surprise—astounded us—by this measure," he later recalled. "But we rose each fighting, grasping whatever he could first reach—a scythe—a pitchfork—a chopping axe, or a butcher's cleaver. We struck in the direction of the sound; and we are rapidly closing in upon him."[19]

Much of his indignation was grounded in the Hamiltonian economic constitutionalism that dominated his early political career. His broad-based reading of the Constitution was rooted in an entrepreneurial ethic of free enterprise and individual pursuit of prosperity, values that were entirely incompatible with slavery's exploitation of labor, and what Lincoln and other Republicans saw as its suppression of the American free enterprise spirit.

On a more political/constitutional level, he objected to Kansas-Nebraska on constitutional grounds, on the relatively narrow basis of how federal authority is allocated. While agreeing with Douglas and other popular sovereignty supporters that local and state governments should make most of the serious, day-to-day decisions involving Americans' lives (including the future of slavery in states where it already existed), he believed that the Constitution gave the federal government special oversight responsibilities for western territories. Popular sovereignty amounted to an abdication of federal power by allowing the first settlers on the scene to forever after determine whether that territory's future included human bondage. Congress should do this in a deliberative fashion, Lincoln believed. Indeed, under the Constitution's provisions that Congress make all laws and rules concerning the territories, it had no choice. During one of his early anti-Nebraska speeches speech in Bloomington, Illinois, Lincoln "held up in a proper light the absurd proposition that Government could lay no restriction upon soil which it had bought and paid for, and over which it exercised a parental care."[20]

Lincoln further fashioned a constitutional objection to popular sovereignty based upon congressional representation. Referring to the famous "three-fifths compromise," by which in 1787 Southerners insisted that their slaves be counted as three-fifths of a person for the purpose of allocating the number of delegates in the House of Representatives, Lincoln pointed out that this arrangement in effect gave white Southern slaveholders more representatives, and thus more power, than they should have in fairness possessed. "The citizens of Slave States, have a political power in the general government beyond their single votes and this violates the equality between American Citizens," he pointed out. Still, Lincoln said, he would have to live with this. "It was 'in the [Constitutional] bond' and he would live faithfully by it."

But now Douglas's popular sovereignty policy meant that a citizen from a free state could, by relocating to a territory and voting for slavery, vote himself into possessing unfair power and influence. Lincoln was "unwilling that his neighbor, living on an equality by his side in Illinois, should by moving over into Kansas be elevated into a state of superiority . . . and become a man and a tenth, whereas before he was formerly only one man . . . !" Perhaps the Founding Fathers had no choice in giving slaveholders an advantage in 1787 with the three-fifths compromise. But it was, according to Lincoln, a certain violation of basic American principles of equality that this advantage be steadily augmented. "If this is 'equal rights' for the Kansas settler," Lincoln declared, then "he would be glad to know what became of his own rights, and the rights of the people of the Free States; while they were thus made into only *fractions of men*, by the creation of *new* Slave States. It is said that the adoption or rejection of slavery in Kansas and Nebraska, concerns the people of those Territories alone—it is no business of ours. This is false. . . . [I]t concerns our dearest rights, our equality with the citizens of those territories—which we are entitled to by every consideration of justice and constitutional guarantees."[21]

But Lincoln found Douglas's handiwork wanting most fundamentally on a moral level. "What *natural* right requires Kansas and
Nebraska to be opened to Slavery?" Lincoln asked. "Is not slavery
universally granted to be, in the abstract, a gross outrage on the law
of nature? Have not all civilized nations, our own among them, made
the Slave trade capital, and classed it with piracy and murder? Is it not
held to be the great wrong of the world?"[22] By allowing at least the possibility that the "gross outrage" of slavery could spread into the West,
popular sovereignty spoke to the worst instincts of slaveholders and
those who wished to become slaveholders—people who either "earn[ed]
their bread from the sweat of other men's faces" or wanted to do so
by moving West and starting new slave-labor farms and institutions.
Kansas-Nebraska was "wrong in its prospective principle, allowing it to
spread to every other part of the wide world, where men can be found
inclined to take it," he declared. Lincoln was particularly incensed
by Douglas's statement that he truly did not care one way or another
whether slavery was voted up or down in the territories, so long as the
votes were counted fairly. Lincoln was appalled. "This *declared* indif-
ference, but as I must think, covert *real* zeal for the spread of slavery, I
can not but hate," Lincoln declared. "I hate it because of the monstrous
injustice of slavery itself. I hate it because it deprives our republican
example of its just influence in the world—enables the enemies of free
institutions, with plausibility, to taunt us as hypocrites—causes the
real friends of freedom to doubt our sincerity, and especially because
it forces so many really good men amongst ourselves into an open war
with the very fundamental principles of civil liberty."[23]

But if Lincoln harbored profound moral objections to the Kansas-
Nebraska Act, he was faced with the problem of how to express those
objections in a concrete way. Lincoln was always a practical man,
rather than a dreamer—it was not in his nature to speak of wispy
abstractions or ideas that weren't anchored in reality. He needed to
craft a new constitutional vision of the United States, potent not
only in its use as a moral weapon to hammer Douglas and popular
sovereignty's supporters in 1854, but also as a constitutional blueprint
for America's future. He needed a constitutional vision that could be
at once practical, politically viable, and morally relevant.

We have seen the essential ingredients of Lincoln's constitutional-ism to this point in his life: His early romanticization of the Constitu-tion and its Founding Father authors, and his robust, Hamiltonian broad constructionism, allowed him to argue for a strong federal government to promote American entrepreneurial energy. We have also seen the limitations on his constitutionalism prior to 1854: his distrust of the document as an instrument of reform, and his belief in a careful, balanced approach to constitutional power. Now Lincoln added in 1854 a new component, one that gave his constitutional vision an added moral impetus while still grounding it in pragma-tism and tapping into the shared reverence felt by Lincoln and his contemporaries for the Revolutionary generation: the Declaration of Independence.

"I have never had a feeling politically that did not spring from the Declaration of Independence," Lincoln would boldly proclaim in 1860. He seems to have been exaggerating here, for prior to 1854 he barely mentioned the Declaration at all. But sometime during the years leading up to the Kansas-Nebraska controversy and his political reawakening, Lincoln connected Thomas Jefferson's ringing declara-tion of human equality to the cause of ending American slavery.

A variety of intellectual influences seem to have come together and pointed Lincoln in the direction of the Declaration. There was of course his veneration of the Framers generally, dating back to his youth. One wonders, too, if Lincoln had read the writings of some antislavery activists—Lysander Spooner, for example—who grounded their critique of slavery in the Declaration and its values.[24]

Whatever its source, Lincoln's invocation of the Declaration was a specific choice, one that flew directly in the face of other Americans (chief justice of the Supreme Court Roger Taney, for example) who went out of their way to limit the Declaration's power and scope as much as possible—the better to place African Americans beyond the pale of its protection. Lincoln's thinking traveled in exactly the opposite direction. His reading of the Declaration was expansive enough to include not only African Americans, but immigrants of different ethnic backgrounds, as well, a position that placed him firmly on the progressive end of antebellum American politics. "Our

Declaration of Independence was held sacred by all, and thought to include all," he declared.[25]

He first made the connection between the Declaration of Independence and the fight against slavery, appropriately enough, during his eulogy of Henry Clay, delivered in early July 1852. After criticizing the radical followers of William Lloyd Garrison, who saw the Constitution as irredeemably proslavery, Lincoln averred that he "would also, if I could, array [Clay's] name, opinions, and influence against the opposite extreme—against a few, but an increasing number of men, who, for the sake of perpetuating slavery, are beginning to assail and to ridicule the white-man's charter of freedom—the declaration that 'all men are created free and equal.'"[26]

Here Lincoln for the first time in his political career used the Declaration of Independence as a tool with which to assail slavery. As he took to the stump two years later in opposition to the Kansas-Nebraska Act, he honed the Declaration into an effective political weapon. He used the document to assail slavery's apologists and Kansas-Nebraska's supporters (for Lincoln, they were one and the same) as betrayers of the Founding Fathers' legacy. "The theory of our government is Universal Freedom," he told a Springfield audience. "'All men are created free and equal,' says the Declaration of Independence." Yet, as he was shocked to learn, some of slavery's more ardent supporters in their zeal to protect human bondage assailed the Declaration, as well. There were even some Northern Democrats, he pointed out, who "pronounced the declaration of independence a self-evident lie." Had someone the temerity to say this at the door to Independence Hall in 1787, Lincoln believed, "the door-keeper would have taken him by the throat and stopped his rascally breath awhile, and then have hurled him into the street."[27]

This was shrewd political strategy, given the sacred place the Revolutionary generation occupied in the hearts of Americans. But Lincoln wanted to use the Declaration for something more than politics. To make his case that the Constitution was a fundamentally antislavery document, Lincoln needed to establish that the Founding Fathers were themselves antislavery, and that they had compromised with slaveholders in drafting the document out of the exigencies of the moment in 1787, hoping all the while to have set the institution on the "path of ultimate extinction."

He did have other weapons besides the Declaration. He often referenced the Northwest Ordinance of 1787, arguing—as had some antislavery activists before him—that the ordinance's ban on slavery spoke of their essential rejection of slavery. "Did not the ordinance of '87 declare that slavery or involuntary servitude, (except as a punishment for crime), *should never exist* in the territory north and west of the Ohio river—the territory out of which have been successively carved the States of Ohio, Indiana, Illinois, Michigan and Wisconsin?" he asked. "And observe its fruits. . . . [N]o States in the world have ever advanced as rapidly in population, wealth, the arts and appliances of life, and now have such promise of prospective greatness, as the very States that were born under the ordinance of '87, and were deprived of the blessings of 'popular sovereignty,' as contained in the Nebraska bill, and without which the people of Kansas and Nebraska cannot get along at all!"[28]

This was a useful argument, and Lincoln returned to it often in his anti-Nebraska speeches. For him, the Northwest Ordinance proved conclusively the antislavery bona fides of the Constitution's Framers; and if the American people were interested in adhering to the Framers' original intent, then they must acknowledge the Framers' antislavery convictions. "This same generation of men, and mostly the same individuals of the generation, who declared this principle—who declared independence—who fought the war of the revolution through—who afterwards made the constitution under which we still live—these same men passed the ordinance of '87, declaring that slavery should never go to the north-west territory," he declared.

Lincoln knew what he was doing, given the fact that nearly all of his fellow Americans in that time period were what modern constitutional scholars call "originalists"; that is, they believed the language of the Constitution was what its authors said it was, no more and no less. Interpreting that language was coterminous with interpreting the Framers' intent. Discover what they wanted, the thinking went, and then one must necessarily discover what the Constitution means. If by using the Northwest Ordinance in this fashion Lincoln could convince his audiences that the Founding Fathers were against slavery, then he would go a long way towards convincing them that the Constitution itself was, at bottom, an antislavery instrument.

Useful as it was, however, the Northwest Ordinance did not resonate with quite the same emotional effect as the Declaration of Independence. The Ordinance did not occupy the same sacred space in Americans' hearts. When he mentioned the Declaration in a speech, he invoked a tone that was reverential, almost mystical. "Our republican robe is soiled, and trailed in the dust" by popular sovereignty and its proslavery supporters, he told listeners in Peoria, Illinois. "Let us repurify it. Let us turn and wash it white, in the spirit, if not the blood, of the Revolution. . . . Let us re-adopt the Declaration of Independence, and with it, the practices, and policy, which harmonize with it. Let north and south—let all Americans—let all lovers of liberty everywhere—join in the great and good work. If we do this, we shall not only have saved the Union; but we shall have so saved it, as to make, and to keep it, forever worthy of the saving."[29]

The Declaration was Lincoln's ace card, his incontrovertible proof that the Founding Fathers wanted slavery dead and gone. "No man is good enough to govern another man, *without that other's consent*," he argued. "I say this is the leading principle—the sheet anchor of American republicanism." Quoting the Declaration's language that "governments are instituted among men, deriving their just powers from the consent of the governed," he continued, "according to our ancient faith, the just powers of governments are derived from the consent of the governed. Now the relation of masters and slaves is . . . a total violation of this principle. The master not only governs the slave without his consent; but he governs him by a set of rules altogether different from those which he prescribes for himself. Allow ALL the governed an equal voice in the government, and that, and that only is self government."[30]

By connecting the Declaration directly to government, rather than the abstract ideal of "all men are created equal," Lincoln located the document in the Constitution's neighborhood. The Constitution was government's blueprint; the Declaration was its heart and soul.

How exactly Lincoln understood the arrangement between the Declaration and the Constitution becomes clear in a little fragment he wrote, apparently for his own private musing, some years after the Kansas-Nebraska controversy, when the nation stood at the doorstep of the Civil War. "Without the *Constitution* and the *Union*, we could not have attained" national prosperity, he wrote, "but even these, are not the primary cause of our great prosperity. There is something back of these, entwining itself more closely about the human heart. That something, is the principle of 'Liberty to all'—the principle that clears the *path* for all—gives *hope* to all—and, by consequence, *enterprise* [sic], and *industry* to all . . . [and] the *expression* of that principle, in our Declaration of Independence, was most happy, and fortunate." He observed that the Declaration had served as a vital unifying influence for the patriots of 1776, for it gave them something tangible around which to rally. "No oppressed, people will *fight*, and *endure*, as our fathers did, without the promise of something better, than a mere change of masters," he believed. Groping for an appropriate metaphor to express what he was trying to say, Lincoln compared the Declaration to an "apple of gold." "The *Union*, and the *Constitution*, are the *picture* of *silver*, subsequently framed around it," he wrote. "The picture was made, not to *conceal*, or *destroy* the apple; but to *adorn*, and *preserve* it. The *picture* was made *for* the apple—*not* the apple for the picture."[31]

The metaphor was Biblical, possibly taken from Proverbs 25:11—"a word fitly spoken is like apples of gold in pictures of silver."[32] Apparently a draft for a speech never given, the fragment's reference to the Declaration as an "apple of gold" and its symbiotic relationship to the Constitution's "frame of silver" did not appear in any of Lincoln's other writings, before or after. But it was in its way a searing little moment of clarity, during which Lincoln found a way to convey, clearly and with pithy simplicity, just what he had been trying to express during those months immediately after Douglas's Kansas-Nebraska proposition so aroused him off his office couch and into action.

In welding the Declaration of Independence to the Constitution—in effect, making the Declaration a constitutional document—Lincoln created a different sort of constitutionalism in American public life. Prior to 1854, Americans were wont to define "constitutionalism" merely along the narrow grounds of federal/state relations, separation of powers within the document, and the strict/broad constructionism debate that had roiled American public life since the days of Alexander Hamilton and Thomas Jefferson.

These were all serious, important constitutional issues, but they were of limited use to a man like Abraham Lincoln: an antislavery man who had to avoid identification with radical abolitionists, but who nevertheless wanted to enter the political fray armed with practical, useful tools to combat the institution of slavery—the greatest moral question of his age. Understanding that arguments on a strictly moral plane could only carry him so far, that indeed the vast majority of white American voters were inclined to reject strictly abstract moral arguments against slavery out of hand due to the prevailing racial prejudice of American life, Lincoln needed a sort of hybrid constitutionalism, one that could appeal at once to the Constitution and to America's innate moral sensibilities. It needed to do so with politically viable, easily recognizable symbols that could be integrated with, rather than set in opposition to, the American constitutional tradition. The Declaration admirably served his purposes.

Invoking the Declaration allowed Lincoln to cut through the endless (and ultimately fruitless) constitutional debates concerning federal/state relations, debates that had ultimately served to perpetuate slavery by robbing America's constitutional conversation of its capacity to directly engage slavery's moral issues. At the same time, Lincoln grounded those moral issues in the Constitution and the quasi-religious political culture surrounding the Founding Fathers, enabling him to function within the American political system in ways that the more radical abolitionists could never do. As the nation careened towards dissolution and civil war, Lincoln's constitutionalism made him a principled, effective, and persuasive antislavery politician.

LINCOLN AND THE DECLARATION
OF INDEPENDENCE

L incoln went to war against slavery after 1854—a political war, primarily, but one that also involved combating the Democratic Party's increasingly proslavery reading of the US Constitution. His primary target was Roger B. Taney, an aging Supreme Court judge who tried to insert proslavery ideology and racism into the very core of the American constitutional tradition, via one of the most infamous Supreme Court decisions in American history: *Dred Scott v. Sandford.*

When Lincoln set his sights on Douglas's Senate seat in 1858, he did so as a member of the brand new Republican Party, formed from ex-Whigs (that party had disintegrated as a national party a few years before), antislavery activists, and those opposed to the Kansas-Nebraska proposal.[1] At first Lincoln was reluctant to join this new party, fearing its association with radical abolitionism, but he need not have worried, at least in terms of the Republicans' actual policies. The new party was moderate in its antislavery aims, wanting only to keep slavery out of the West while allowing white Southerners to deal with the institution in their own time and manner. "Let us withdraw from [slavery] the protection of our federal government, leave it to itself, and it will at once decline and at length die," argued one Republican newspaper editor.[2]

Lincoln's new party, like Lincoln himself, was antislavery, but not especially committed to the pursuit of racial equality. Still, despite these limitations, there was potential in Lincoln's Declaration-centered constitutionalism—potential for Lincoln, the Republicans, and even Americans generally to someday rise above the muck of white supremacy. In that same Monticello speech during which he proclaimed his desire not to pursue "negro equality in all things," Lincoln quickly added "*he only wanted that the words* of the Declaration of Independence should be applied, to wit: 'That all men are created free and equal.'"[3]

Just what he meant by this Lincoln kept vague, probably purposely so, pursuing a shrewd politician's strategy of speaking words that could be interpreted in slightly different ways by different constituents. But all could understand two basic truths: First, however unclear his definition of "equal" might be, it did include, in some fashion, African Americans; and second, this was farther than Stephen Douglas and his fellow Democrats were willing to go.

Despite the Republicans' repeated and loud protestations that such sentiments did not in any way make them abolitionists, Democrats pounced on the opportunity to paint their new opponents as dangerous promoters of racial equality. "Black Republican" was the common label affixed by Democrats to Lincoln's party, a none-too-subtle allusion that Republicans wanted social, political, and even sexual mixing of the races. The Republicans "know, or ought to know, that in their own ranks were not only to be found Free-Soilers but Abolitionists," thundered a typical Democratic Party bromide. "Yes sir, the lowest and most God-forsaken, nigger-stealing Abolitionists were to be found . . . doing battle against the national Democracy, side by side with . . . the leaders of the Black Republican party."[4]

For their part, white Southerners wanted the Constitution used as a bulwark for the protection of slave owners' property. The slaves, argued one Southern congressman, "were considered by the laws of the States as a species of animals. . . . [And] the Constitution, having thus found them, left them to be considered by the States as property of a peculiar character." Far from seeing Lincoln's antislavery Declaration of Independence at its center, Southerners believed the Constitution's primary purpose was to guarantee their right to keep that peculiar "property," and to carry it with them westwards whenever they saw fit to do so. "The South should establish . . . the principle that the right of a southern man to his slave is equal, in its length and breadth, to the right of a Northern man to his horse," bluntly argued Congressman Laurence Keitt of South Carolina; "she should make the recognition of the right full, complete, and indisputable."[5]

This proslavery reading of the Constitution received a big boost in 1857, when the US Supreme Court announced its decision in the case of *Dred Scott v. Sandford*.

The immediate question before the court concerned the fate of Dred Scott, the slave of an army physician who during the late 1830s took Scott with him on military assignments in Illinois and Wisconsin (present-day Minnesota) territory. When the doctor returned to the army's Jefferson Barracks, located in St. Louis, Missouri—a slave state—Scott sued for his freedom, claiming that his sojourns on Illinois and Wisconsin's free soil made him a free man who could not be reenslaved. The case was complex, involving years of litigation in the lower state and federal courts.[6]

The Supreme Court's chief justice was seventy-nine-year-old Roger B. Taney, a longtime Democrat and a Maryland slaveholder. Taney was reputed to be a moderate who in his younger days expressed doubts about the peculiar institution, calling it "a blot on our national character." More generally, Taney enjoyed a sterling reputation as an excellent judge. "He has discharged the duties of [chief justice] with an ability and impartiality worthy of the illustrious judges who had preceded him upon the bench," read a typical assessment published the same year the court handed down the *Dred Scott* ruling.[7]

But whatever he may have once thought about slavery as a "blot," his rulings from the bench related to slavery consistently supported the institution. He also disliked and feared the new Republican Party and the specter of sectionalism and racial strife he believed it represented. "The provision incorporated into the Constitution for the special protection of the peculiar institution, on which the present prosperity and safety of the Southern States depended, was openly and persistently violated and nullified" by antislavery Northerners, Taney later claimed, and the Republicans were nothing more than tools of abolitionist radicals who formed "a party breathing this sectional spirit."[8]

This being the case, it is not surprising that Dred Scott lost his bid for freedom. Speaking for a seven-to-two majority of the court, Taney ruled that Scott's temporary sojourns on the free soil of Wisconsin and Illinois were irrelevant to his status. "As Scott was a slave when taken into the State of Illinois by his owner, and was there held as such, and brought back in that character, his status, as free or slave, depended on the laws of Missouri, and not of Illinois," Taney argued. Since Missouri was a slave state, Scott's legal status was therefore unchanged.[9]

Had Taney stopped there, the *Dred Scott* case might never have generated much controversy. But the chief justice was hunting bigger game than the fate of one black man. He ruled that Scott's case should never have been heard in the first place, because only American citizens could bring lawsuits in an American court. "We think they [African Americans] are not, and that they are not included, and were not intended to be included, under the word 'citizens' in the Constitution," he ruled, "and can therefore claim none of the rights and privileges which that instrument provides for and secures to citizens of the United States. On the contrary, they were at that time [the framing of the Constitution] considered as a subordinate and inferior class of beings, who had been subjugated by the dominant race, and, whether emancipated or not, yet remained subject to their authority, and had no rights or privileges but such as those who held the power and the Government might choose to grant them."

"Whether emancipated or not" . . . that was an important and disturbing little phrase. Taney's belief that black people were not citizens rested not just on their status as slaves, but rather on the fact that they were black. He went out of his way to slam shut the constitutional door loudly and firmly in the faces of African Americans. They "had no rights which the white man was bound to respect," Taney infamously asserted; "the negro might justly and lawfully be reduced to slavery for his benefit. He was bought and sold, and treated as an ordinary article of merchandise and traffic, whenever a profit could be made by it."

But what about the Declaration of Independence—Lincoln's apple of gold that created an American tradition rooted in human freedom and liberty without regard to skin color? Nonsense, Taney ruled. "The general words [of the Declaration's preamble] would seem to embrace the whole human family," Taney admitted. "But it is too clear for dispute, that the enslaved African race were not intended to be included, and formed no part of the people who framed and adopted this declaration."

Dred Scott v. Sandford was nothing less than a judicial ratification of American racial prejudice, burning bigotry directly and indelibly into the fabric of the Constitution itself. In reaching this conclusion, Taney in fact badly misrepresented 1787; as his critics (including Justice Benjamin Curtis, who wrote a strong dissent) noted, there were numerous examples of Revolutionary-era Americans affording black people in some states basic legal and civil rights, and the question of whether or not the Framers wanted to design a lily-white American constitutional tradition was very much open to question, then and now. But Taney ignored this fact and devoted considerable attention and historical research to his premise that the Constitution was rooted in white supremacy and was entirely compatible with the wishes and aims of white Southern slaveholders. Citing in particular the Constitution's protection of the slave trade until 1808 in the provisions of Article II, Section 9, and Article IV, Section 2 requiring the return of escaped slaves, Taney concluded that these clauses "point directly and specifically to the negro race as a separate class of persons, and show clearly that they were not regarded as a portion of the people or citizens of the Government then formed." Moreover, according to Taney, black people forever after 1787 were excluded from the American body politic. "Neither the description of persons therein referred to, nor their descendants," he argued, "were embraced in any of the other provisions of the Constitution; for certainly these two clauses were not intended to confer on them or their posterity the blessings of liberty, or any of the personal rights so carefully provided for the citizen."

When he turned to the vexing matter of slavery's status in the western territories, Taney again sided with slaveholders. Using the same Fifth Amendment clause Republicans employed to justify keeping slavery out of the West, he focused not on the amendment's guarantee of "life" and "liberty" but rather "property." "Thus the rights of property are united with the rights of person, and placed on the same ground by the fifth amendment to the Constitution, which provides that no person shall be deprived of life, liberty, and property, without due process of law," he ruled, "and an act of Congress which deprives a citizen of the United States of his liberty or property, merely because he came himself or brought his property into a particular Territory of the United States, and who had committed no offence against the laws, could hardly be dignified with the name of due process of law."

The Missouri Compromise line was now rendered unconstitutional, as was popular sovereignty, for from Taney's perspective both of those measures sought to unconstitutionally interpose government authority—either in drawing a geographic line, or authorizing a referendum on slavery—between citizens and the Fifth Amendment, which guaranteed their rights. "If the Constitution recognises [*sic*] the right of property of the master in a slave, and makes no distinction between that description of property and other property owned by a citizen, no tribunal, acting under the authority of the United States, whether it be legislative, executive, or judicial, has a right to draw such a distinction, or deny to it the benefit of the provisions and guarantees which have been provided for the protection of private property against the encroachments of the Government."[10]

Slaveholders everywhere rejoiced, for Taney had given them a clear-cut legal victory and a touchstone for buttressing any future arguments about the Constitution's proslavery character or the inferiority of black Americans. Northerners, on the other hand, were stunned, with Republicans and abolitionists naturally leading the way. "In every fiber of my soul I loath and abhor the 'Dred Scott decision,'" seethed an antislavery pastor from New York. "If the Dred Scott decision is good law, [then] the question of slavery or freedom in this country is irrevocably settled," bemoaned a Maine congressman; "the Constitution which the builders constructed is already overthrown, and the Union for liberty and republicanism which rested thereon exists no longer." Even foreign observers were shocked. Quoting the "no rights a white person is bound to respect" portion of the decision, a British writer fumed that "the language fails to convey the full meaning of the awful denunciation; the rights of a whole race, annihilated by a Constitution and a Declaration, commencing with the words 'All men are born free and equal!'"[11]

Some of the anger directed at the Supreme Court took extreme forms; a few Northerners darkly called for open resistance to the law, and even secession from a Union that included slaveholding zealots. Lincoln and his fellow Republicans were entirely unwilling to go so far, wanting instead for Northerners to overturn *Dred Scott* and its proslavery politics at the ballot box.[12]

Lincoln took particular issue—predictably enough—with Taney's constricted reading of the Declaration of Independence. As Lincoln saw it, the chief justice had argued "that the authors of [the Declaration] did not intend to include negroes, by the fact that they did not at once, actually place them on an equality with the whites." But now, Lincoln pointed out, "this grave argument comes to just nothing at all, by the other fact, that they did not at once, *or ever afterwards*, actually place all white people on an equality with one or another." For Lincoln, the Declaration was all about potential. "They did not mean to assert the obvious untruth, that all were then [in 1776] actually enjoying that equality, nor yet, that they were about to confer it immediately upon them. In fact they had no power to confer such a boon. They meant simply to declare the *right*, so that the *enforcement* of it might follow as fast as circumstances should permit. They meant to set up a standard maxim for free society, which should be familiar to all, and revered by all; constantly looked to, constantly labored for, and even though never perfectly attained, constantly approximated, and thereby constantly spreading and deepening its influence, and augmenting the happiness and value of life to all people of all colors everywhere."[13]

But however much resonance this approach might have carried politically, it did Lincoln little good on a constitutional level. Even if he convinced all the voters within earshot that his was the proper interpretation of the Declaration and the Constitution, it would not change the fact that Taney's interpretation carried the heavy force of law.

Taney had, after all, rooted his decision in the deepest available soil—the Supreme Court's power of judicial review, which dated all the way back to the early days of the republic. Chief Justice John Marshall ruled in the 1803 case of *Marbury v. Madison* that the Supreme Court was the final arbiter of constitutional language and its meaning. Presidents and congressmen wrangled over the politics of policymaking, while the Supreme Court decided whether or not the politicians and their policies squared with the Constitution. The court was the final word on the subject, to be gainsaid by no one. By Lincoln's day, this doctrine carried all the power that tradition and over a half-century's worth of practice could confer. Americans by and large were comfortable with judicial review; anyone who questioned it, or called for open defiance of a court ruling, ran the risk of being labeled an anarchist.[14]

Lincoln understood this. "We think [the Supreme Court's] decisions on Constitutional questions, when fully settled, should control, not only the particular cases decided, but the general policy of the country," he told a Springfield audience, "subject to be disturbed only by amendments of the Constitution as provided in that instrument itself. More than this would be revolution."[15]

The key caveat here, however, lay in the words "when fully settled." Court decisions derived their constitutional authority, Lincoln argued, not merely by virtue of the fact that the court handed down a decision, but by that decision's accumulated weight of logic, tradition, and practice. "Judicial decisions are of greater or less authority as precedents, according to circumstances," he pointed out, and such circumstances needed to be more than merely the opinion of a bare court majority at a given moment in time. That opinion had to carry with it the weight of other factors. "If [*Dred Scott*] had been made by the unanimous concurrence of the judges, and without any apparent partisan bias, and in accordance with legal public expectation, and with the steady practice of the departments throughout our history," Lincoln declared, "or, if wanting in some of these, it had been before the court more than once, and had there been affirmed and re-affirmed through a course of years, it then might be, perhaps would be, factious, nay, even revolutionary, to not acquiesce in it as a precedent."[16]

But none of this was true where *Dred Scott* was concerned. Lincoln saw in that decision little more than the capricious will of one angry old man who happened to be at the helm of the nation's highest tribunal. Taney's ruling flew directly in the face of logic, tradition, and the American moral code imbedded within the Declaration of Independence. *Dred Scott* was idiosyncratic, an aberration, "an astonisher in legal history," he argued.[17] The Supreme Court did possess the legal authority to keep Dred Scott himself in bondage, and the court possessed the power, first enumerated by John Marshall, to review and pass judgment on the meaning of the Constitution. But if a given decision was not rooted in consensus—both within the court and with the other branches—and a proper respect for history and tradition, then that decision should not be binding on the rest of the nation and should not be considered the final word on the subject. Other branches of the government could, and should, pursue policies that ran entirely counter to the *Dred Scott* decision. "If I were in Congress, and a vote should come up on a question whether slavery should be prohibited in a new territory, in spite of that Dred Scott decision, I would vote that it should," Lincoln asserted.[18]

In a way, Lincoln's argument was a species of the political tail wagging the constitutional dog. The Republican Party had carefully fashioned a middle-ground antislavery position for itself by condemning slavery's spread into the western territories without mounting an assault on the institution where it already existed. That middle ground was good politics; Lincoln needed to protect it by undermining *Dred Scott*, and so he fashioned a constitutional argument to fit that political need.

But he was motivated by principle as well as politics: namely, that the exercise of power in the American republic must be accompanied by due attention to consequences, and to relevant factors of reason, tradition, and historical practice. The will of a lone government official, no matter how highly placed—even the chief justice of the nation's highest tribunal—meant little if that will was used to exercise power in an arbitrary fashion.

What Lincoln really questioned in his critique of the *Dred Scott* decision was not so much the court's power of judicial review, but more so its legitimacy. Taney could keep a black man in bondage; the chief justice had the power to do that. But his power was not accompanied by persuasive logic, and it was rooted in a faulty reading of the nation's founding documents and their historical context. As such, *Dred Scott* lacked the qualities required for the other branches of the government, and the American people as a whole, to give it the decisive and long-lasting respect of definitive constitutional authority—of legitimacy.

As the 1858 Illinois Senate race heated up, Douglas publicly endorsed the *Dred Scott* decision. He really had no other choice. Southern Democrats expected as much, and he needed them for his upcoming presidential nomination bid in 1860. "The Democracy of Illinois, in the first place, accepts the decision of the Supreme Court of the United States in the case of Dred Scott, as an authoritative interpretation of the Constitution," he told a New Orleans audience in 1858; "in accordance with that decision, we hold that slaves are property, and hence on an equality with all other kinds of property, and that the owner of a slave has the same right to move into a territory with him, as the owner of any other kind of property has to go there and carry his property with him."[19]

This sounded good in the abstract. But the essence of popular sovereignty was the voters' power in western territories to keep slavery from their midst via the ballot box. Unfortunately for Douglas, the *Dred Scott* decision now held this unconstitutional. Party politics forced Douglas to back Taney, but in doing so he undermined the doctrine of popular sovereignty that was now indelibly associated with his name and was also the foundation of his political future.

Lincoln was happy to exploit this dilemma. He wondered how the Little Giant could possibly endorse both *Dred Scott* and popular sovereignty when the court case rendered popular sovereignty unconstitutional by holding that no government measure could interfere with the right to owning slave property. "Under the Dred Scott decision, 'squatter sovereignty' squatted out of existence," he joked. Lincoln also made it a point of contention during their 1858 election contest for the US Senate. At their second debate in Freeport, Illinois, Lincoln posed two questions for Douglas to answer: "Can the people of a United States Territory, in any lawful way, against the wish of any citizen of the United States, exclude slavery from its limits prior to the formation of a State Constitution?" and "If the Supreme Court of the United States shall decide that States can not exclude slavery from their limits, are you in favor of acquiescing in, adopting and following such decision as a rule of political action?[20]

What was Douglas to do? When he stood up in Freeport to reply to Lincoln, he argued that the people of a territory could mount an end run around the Supreme Court's judicial review power by use of local laws. "In my opinion the people of a territory can, by lawful means, exclude slavery from their limits prior to the formation of a State Constitution," Douglas retorted; "the people have the lawful means to introduce it or exclude it as they please, for the reason that slavery cannot exist a day or an hour anywhere, unless it is supported by local police regulations. Those police regulations can only be established by the local legislature, and if the people are opposed to slavery they will elect representatives to that body who will by unfriendly legislation effectually prevent the introduction of it into their midst. If, on the contrary, they are for it, their legislation will favor its extension. Hence, no matter what the decision of the Supreme Court may be on that abstract question, still the right of the people to make a slave territory or a free territory is perfect and complete under the Nebraska bill."[21]

Thus did Stephen Douglas articulate what came to be known as the Freeport Doctrine. Lincoln was not impressed. "When all the trash, the words, the collateral matter was cleared away from it," Lincoln averred, and when "all the chaff was fanned out of it, it was a bare absurdity—*no less than a thing may be lawfully driven away from where it has a lawful right to be.* Clear it of all the verbiage, and that is the naked truth of his proposition."[22]

The judgment of history also has not been favorable. Historian David Potter called the Freeport Doctrine the "lame expedient of telling the South that it possessed constitutional rights which it could not enforce, and the North that it had constitutional obligations which it need not fulfill." There is also a longstanding tradition that in proffering such an argument Douglas permanently alienated Southern Democrats, who would tolerate only a complete and unqualified endorsement of *Dred Scott.* Some have even argued that the ever-savvy Lincoln planted his question as a sort of time bomb, rigged to go off two years later during the 1860 presidential election, when it would cost the Little Giant crucial support in the South. "Gentlemen, I am after bigger game," Lincoln reportedly told his advisors. "If Douglas answers, he can never be president."[23]

This scenario gives Lincoln too much credit for what would have been truly unbelievable prescience; besides, on a purely political level, what Douglas said made sense. He had more reason for concern over the future of Northern Democrats than he did the South's ire, about which he could do relatively little ("He cares nothing for the South," Lincoln wrote to a friend; "he knows he is already dead there").[24] The Freeport Doctrine gave Douglas and other Northern Democrats plausible cover for holding the seemingly contradictory opinion that both *Dred Scott* and popular sovereignty were compatible. In the process he also managed to reaffirm his and his party's commitment to local autonomy and self government, something dear to the hearts of most American voters.

But there truly was no way to square *Dred Scott* with popular sovereignty without doing serious damage to the Constitution itself. Leaving aside the particular context of Douglas's doctrine—slavery, the territories, and the Senate election of 1858—there was a general principle at the heart of the Freeport Doctrine, disturbing in its implications: that local Americans could, through willful noncompliance, subvert a right protected by Constitution. This principle would, if put into practice, have seriously hamstrung federal authority.

But if Douglas faced an intractable problem in *Dred Scott*'s relationship to popular sovereignty, Lincoln likewise faced his own problems with his Declaration-centered "apple of gold" constitutionalism. The Supreme Court of the United States had gone out of its way to cut the rug from underneath Lincoln's reading of the Declaration, arguing that the golden apple applied to whites only. But even more problematic was the fact that Lincoln's doctrine sounded rather suspiciously like an endorsement of racial equality in America.

The Abraham Lincoln of the 1850s was not much of a racial egalitarian. But in the hothouse racial climate of the day, the barest intimation that he harbored such sentiments was a political kiss of death. Lincoln well knew this, as did Douglas, and he was not about to let Illinois's voters forget it. The Little Giant hammered away at this point: A vote for Abraham Lincoln was a vote for racial equality. Douglas's tone was ugly. "Mr. Lincoln, following the example and lead of all the little Abolition orators, who go around and lecture in the basements of schools and churches, reads from the Declaration of Independence, that all men were created equal," he told the crowd during their first debate in Ottawa, Illinois. "I do not question Mr. Lincoln's conscientious belief that the negro was made his equal, and hence is his brother, but for my own part, I do not regard the negro as my equal, and positively deny that he is my brother or any kin to me whatever. . . . Now, I do not believe that the Almighty ever intended the negro to be the equal of the white man. If he did, he has been a long time demonstrating the fact. For thousands of years the negro has been a race upon the earth, and during all that time, in all latitudes and climates, wherever he has wandered or been taken, he has been inferior to the race which he has there met. He belongs to an inferior race, and must always occupy an inferior position."[25]

However nasty Douglas's tone may have been, it sounded a responsive chord among Illinois's lily-white electorate. The state was renowned for its repressive laws directed specifically at excluding and discriminating against African Americans; when Douglas attacked black people, he was simply going mainstream. His remarks were often met with cheers, and his racial jokes at Lincoln's expense brought forth the very sort of laughter from his listeners that Douglas wanted. "All I have to say of it is this, that if you, Black Republicans, think that the negro ought to be on a social equality with your wives and daughters, and ride in a carriage with your wife, whilst you drive the team, you have a perfect right to do so," Douglas shouted during their Freeport debate. Warming to the subject, Douglas continued: "All I have to say on that subject is that those of you who believe that the negro is your equal and ought to be on an equality with you socially, politically, and legally; have a right to entertain those opinions, and of course will vote for Mr. Lincoln," after which the crowd shouted "down with the negro."[26]

Such was the atmosphere Lincoln faced as he and Douglas toured seven towns up and down Illinois throughout the summer and early fall of 1858. Some towns were more receptive to Douglas's tactics than others. The Little Giant himself complained that Lincoln and his party professed more egalitarian impulses in the northern part of the state than they did in the southern section (nicknamed "Egypt"), which hosted more emigrants from the slave South. Lincoln and the Republicans "do not hoist the same flag; they do not own the same principles, or profess the same faith," Douglas complained during their debate in Jonesboro. Nevertheless, Lincoln faced a white voting electorate in Illinois that was more or less uniformly hostile to any suggestion of equality between white and black Americans.[27]

He accordingly backpedaled from any suggestion that either he or his party had ever endorsed racial equality. "I have no purpose to introduce political and social equality between the white and the black races," he declared. "There is a physical difference between the two, which in my judgment will probably forever forbid their living together upon the footing of perfect equality, and inasmuch as it becomes a necessity that there must be a difference, I, as well as Judge Douglas, am in favor of the race to which I belong, having the superior position."[28]

Lincoln was here bowing to the realities of his times; an example of his aforementioned hedging on the question of racial equality (note the qualifiers "probably" and "inasmuch as it becomes a necessity"). But whatever his language and his meaning, it belonged within the realm of *politics*, the give-and-take of the ever-present battle to gain votes and hold public office in American democracy.

It was not, however, *constitutionalism*: statements of fundamental principles rooted in America's founding documents. On that level, Lincoln did not retreat in the face of Douglas's vitriol. He remained remarkably consistent throughout his debates with the Little Giant.

Lincoln's detractors have fairly pounced on his claim that he had "no purpose to introduce political and social equality between the white and the black races" as proof positive of his supposed bigotry and lack of commitment to racial equality. But those same critics often omit the words Lincoln spoke shortly afterwards, right after reassuring the audience that he, "as well as Judge Douglas, am in favor of the race to which I belong, having the superior position." For he then stated that "notwithstanding all this, there is no reason in the world why the negro is not entitled to all the natural rights enumerated in the Declaration of Independence, the right to life, liberty and the pursuit of happiness. I hold that he is as much entitled to these as the white man. I agree with Judge Douglas he is not my equal in many respects—certainly not in color, perhaps not in moral or intellectual endowment. But in the right to eat the bread, without leave of anybody else, which his own hand earns, *he is my equal and the equal of Judge Douglas, and the equal of every living man.*"[29]

Lincoln worked this theme time and again, both during the debates and afterwards: Douglas and his supporters were engaged in a disturbing campaign to gut the Declaration of its original, inclusive meaning and purpose—the eventual demise of slavery. "If they would repress all tendencies to liberty and ultimate emancipation, they must go back to the era of our independence and muzzle the cannon which thundered its annual joyous return on the Fourth of July; they must blow out the moral lights around us; they must penetrate the human soul and eradicate the love of liberty," Lincoln declared. In so doing, Douglas and his supporters would dehumanize African Americans, "teaching that the negro is no longer a man but a brute; that the Declaration has nothing to do with him; that he ranks with the crocodile and the reptile; that man, with body and soul, is a matter of dollars and cents."[30]

Going beyond altruism, Lincoln appealed to his white voters' self-interest. Today, Douglas reads African Americans out of the Declaration, Lincoln pointed out; tomorrow, they could be next. "When you have stricken down the principles of the Declaration of Independence, and thereby consigned the negro to hopeless and eternal bondage, are you *quite* sure that the demon will not turn and rend you?" he asked an audience in Bloomington, Illinois. "Will not the people then be ready to go down beneath the tread of any tyrant who may wish to rule them?"[31]

Properly understood, Lincoln's Declaration afforded African Americans, along with everyone else, the potential for future betterment and achievement. It gave the African American a basic, sacred right to earn, to progress, and to improve. More generally, the Declaration of Independence created a high ideal, embodying the natural rights of all people, towards which the American system—embodied in the legal and political machinery of the Constitution—was geared to strive.

Lincoln always conceded that the Constitution and its system of laws afforded white Southerners certain basic protection in their slaveholding rights. "I confess I hate to see the poor creatures hunted down, and caught, and carried back to their stripes, and unrewarded toils; but I bite my lip and keep quiet," Lincoln wrote to a friend from Kentucky. While on the political circuit, he told his audiences that he conceded white Southerners' constitutional rights to own slaves, and to have those slaves returned to them when they ran away. "When [Southerners] remind us of their constitutional rights, I acknowledge them, not grudgingly, but fully, and fairly," he declared, "and I would give them any legislation for the reclaiming of their fugitives, which should not, in its stringency, be more likely to carry a free man into slavery, than our ordinary criminal laws are to hang an innocent one."[32]

But if he wasn't grudging in his recognition of slaveholders' rights, neither was he terribly enthusiastic. That recognition was necessary, he knew. "Thus, the thing is hid away, in the constitution, just as an afflicted man hides away a wen or a cancer, which he dares not cut out at once, lest he bleed to death; with the promise, nevertheless, that the cutting may begin at the end of a given time," Lincoln claimed. Where Roger Taney's Founding Fathers were enthusiastic and unrepentant slavers and bigots, Lincoln's Founders were reluctant enablers of an institution that they secretly detested. "Necessity drove them so far, and farther, they would not go. . . . They hedged and hemmed it in to the narrowest limits of necessity."[33]

The Declaration redeemed this unfortunate state of affairs. It was the only assurance that the cancer would not grow, or even remain intact. The Declaration was like a team of horses yoked to the Constitution's wagon, a wagon that by necessity and its own construction sometimes hindered the horses' forward progress, but which in turn required that progress if it were to advance at all. "Negroes have natural rights however, as other men have," Lincoln argued; "[the Declaration] does not declare that all men are equal in their attainments or social position, yet no sane man will attempt to deny that the African upon his own soil has all the natural rights that instrument vouchsafes to all mankind."[34]

As a statement of politics, Lincoln's Declaration-centered constitutionalism was a limited doctrine. It did little to improve African-Americans' lot in the here and now of 1858, and it conceded that African Americans would remain second-class citizens. Lincoln would not take a quixotic tilt at racism's impregnable windmill, at least not in 1858. "I believe the declara[tion] that 'all men are created equal' is the great fundamental principle upon which our free institutions rest," he wrote, "but it does not follow that social and political equality between whites and blacks, *must* be incorporated, because slavery must *not*. The declaration does not so require."[35]

Likewise as a matter of his personal convictions concerning race and racial equality, Lincoln's statements are carefully circumscribed, and confusing. Even today, it is difficult to tell whether or not Lincoln really believed in the possibility of a racially diverse America. He may have chosen to conceal, as a matter of political expediency, a private conviction that someday at least slavery would disappear and be replaced by some measure of racial equality. Or, he may have been genuinely troubled and skeptical about even the barest possibility of a racially diverse America.

His statements in 1858 are limited on personal and political levels. But as a statement of basic principles, his language reveals a legitimate commitment to a constitutionalism that carried within itself the promise of progress. To his mind, the Declaration did not commit the nation to enacting racial equality in 1858; it did, however, commit the nation to a timeless, universal principle of human equality towards which Americans could and should strive.

Here was a potent doctrine, particularly compared to the fossilized originalism of Roger Taney's constitutionalism, which would have permanently defined Americans according to the worst racist angels of their natures. Taney's constitutionalism was the wagon without the horses. By comparison, Lincoln's vision was evolutionary, carrying the potential for future, fundamental change.

His Declaration-centered constitutionalism also demonstrates a gulf of intellect and principle between himself and Stephen Douglas. When confronted with a difficult constitutional problem—how to reconcile *Dred Scott* with popular sovereignty—the Little Giant articulated a solution that was politically expedient but constitutionally unworkable. Lincoln, on the other hand, showed that he was willing to stand upon a consistent constitutional doctrine even when doing so might cost him votes. He seemed to pander politically to the racism of his day by declaring his noncommitment to racial equality; but he also simultaneously told white voters, despite the censure of the Supreme Court and Stephen Douglas and the pervasive racism of the day, that the Declaration of Independence certainly did apply to black people.

It was the measure of the man. It showed that Lincoln was indeed quite a bit taller than the Little Giant—and Roger Taney.

CHAPTER FOUR

BECOMING PRESIDENT AND
DEFENDING THE UNION

Roger Taney made Lincoln president—at least in a literal sense. As the Supreme Court's chief justice, he administered the oath of office, a task he had performed for eight presidents over twenty-five years. He did the deed one last time on the afternoon of March 4, 1861. The ceremony came off without a hitch, though some saw hints of the old man's disdain for Lincoln, the first president elected from the new party he despised, the Republicans. Taney "seemed very agitated" during the oath, thought one observer, "and his hands shook perceptively with emotion."[1]

People underestimated president-elect Lincoln, often because they knew so little about him. The national press couldn't even get the spelling of his first name right, routinely substituting "Abram" for "Abraham," much to Lincoln's annoyance. The barebones outline of his life served up during the campaign—rail-splitter and poor farmer's son, self-educated frontier attorney—invited contempt in some circles. William Seward, for example, who was one of Lincoln's rivals for the Republican nomination (and soon to become Lincoln's secretary of state), privately disparaged his new boss as nothing more than a "little Illinois lawyer" and assumed he would easily be able to manipulate Lincoln to his own ends.[2]

But Lincoln was no hillbilly. He possessed a keen and searching intellect, more so than might have been expected from a man of such humble beginnings and limited education. He had his collection of folksy anecdotes and stories, to be sure, which he trotted out on any occasion. But he also read widely—everything from texts on trigonometry to Shakespeare—and with more depth and understanding than many realized. "Any man who took Lincoln for a simple minded man would very soon wake [up] with his back in a ditch," recalled a friend.[3]

His approach to the Constitution was likewise far from simple. He developed in his Declaration-centered constitutionalism an approach well suited to the times, and in keeping with his instincts as an antislavery moderate. The symbiotic relationship he proposed between the Declaration of Independence and the US Constitution allowed him to assault the institution of slavery while preserving fidelity to the nation's legal and political system. He harbored some conservative tendencies, most notably his deep respect for law and order and his reverence for the Revolutionary generation. These tendencies stood him in good stead: they rooted him, anchoring his ideas in tradition and an abiding sense of history. But his Declaration-centered constitutionalism was fundamentally progressive and forward looking.

War was an unexpected, unwelcome, and largely unforeseen circumstance that would test this constitutional vision. The truth is that Lincoln had actually never given much thought to war at all. The subject of war surfaced in his antebellum political career on only one occasion, when Congressman Lincoln spoke out against President James K. Polk's pursuit of war with Mexico in 1846. His opposition was rooted in politics and a moral questioning of the president's actions more than any serious analysis of Polk's constitutional war-making powers. Lincoln voted in favor of a Whig resolution claiming the president had begun the war "unnecessarily and unconstitutionally," but neither he nor the resolution's authors were specific about their constitutional objections. Lincoln did not mention the Constitution in either his "spot resolutions" of December 1847 (in which he questioned the "spot" of soil upon which Polk claimed Mexican soldiers attacked the American army) or later in his congressional speech on the subject.[4]

Most Americans gave only sporadic attention to the constitutional questions of waging war prior to 1860, because between the

Revolution and the Civil War, the country did not experience a war that held the nation's attention long enough to seriously examine the Constitution's war-making mechanisms.

Just what were those mechanisms?

First, there was the constitutional machinery for starting a war, which gave the president enough room to fire the first shot, but contemplated eventual congressional action in formally declaring that a state of war existed. The Framers were not precise concerning the proper balance between the president and Congress here, and there was plenty of room for argument over just how a war should get started, and how long it should continue before the people's representatives in Congress became more actively involved.

Assuming there could be a war, which branch of the federal government possessed the requisite constitutional authority to administer and prosecute it? Article II names the president as commander in chief of the armed forces, while Article I empowers Congress to raise those forces and fund them, and to make the rules governing their conduct and administration. This sort of divided power is a classic example of American constitutionalism's separation of powers, splitting and diluting authority among the branches so that no one person or group of people in government could get too much power and beget tyranny.[5]

Protection from tyranny came at the expense of efficiency, however, because the line of war-making authority between president and Congress was murky, at best. As commander in chief, the president exercised direct operational control of the nation's armed forces. He could issue orders to commanding officers, call out and take command of state militia forces, and even theoretically take the field and lead soldiers directly into combat. In the name of enforcing the Constitution's obligation to collect uniform duties throughout the entire United States, and his power to suppress insurrection, Lincoln could (and did) impose a naval blockade on Southern ports. The blockade was controversial under international law—if the Confederacy was not a bona fide nation, then Lincoln's blockade seemed to be, in effect, a nation blockading itself—but not so much under the US Constitution.

In practice, presidents commanded the armed forces through the secretary of war, an officer not contemplated by the Constitution; and it was generally understood that, following the time-honored American tradition of civilian control over the military, that the secretary in turn possessed supervisory power over the commanding officers of the army and navy.

The president, the secretary of war, the generals and admirals in charge of the army and navy—on paper the chain of command looked clear-cut, and it had worked well enough during the relatively small, brief wars the nation had fought since 1787. But how would it function in a large-scale, lengthy conflict? Also, where exactly did Congress fit in? Article I, Section 8 empowers Congress to perform some specific military tasks, such as establishing rules for the capture of foreign vessels on the high seas, and arming and training militia soldiers. It also grants Congress broad-based powers: "to raise and support Armies," and "to make rules for the government and regulation of the land and naval forces." Much discretion lay within that language. While no one contemplated its involvement in day-to-day combat operations or command decisions, Congress's constitutional prerogative to "make rules" and "regulate" the military could be construed as a license to investigate and if necessary discipline soldiers who failed to perform their duties properly. At the very least, Congress's power of the purse over military expenditures gave it potentially powerful leverage over the army, the navy, the civilians who contracted to provide supplies, and possibly the president himself, whose powers as commander in chief meant little if Congress refused to approve expenditures for the weapons necessary to carry out his commands.[6]

The Supreme Court might have been expected to step in and clarify some of these matters. But the court is the branch of the federal government with the fewest direct ties to the nation's military establishment. Article III stipulates almost no wartime role for the court, and over the years, it has had fewer members with a military background than either Congress or the presidency. The court accordingly has proven reluctant to involve itself in military issues.[7]

This being the case, war-making was primarily a function shared between the president and Congress. But nothing was explicitly spelled out in the Constitution concerning the various potential flashpoints between those two branches. The Constitution is after all only scaffolding upon which subsequent generations of Americans have erected the details of the national structure as they have seen fit. Trouble was that in 1860, the war-making scaffolding was especially bare. Lincoln and the American people would be forced to erect the legal and constitutional structure of a very big war on the fly, often improvising to meet rapidly changing circumstances, all while under the tremendous pressure of fighting for the nation's very existence.

This was true not only for matters related to the battle front; the home front created daunting constitutional problems, as well, because in a civil war there often is no clear line delineating friend and enemy. Lincoln had to distinguish between those who expressed a healthy loyal opposition to his administration's policies, and those whose opposition might cripple the war effort from within.

His precise constitutional authority to seek such distinctions lay in the language of Article II, Section I outlining his oath of office: "I do solemnly swear (or affirm) that I will faithfully execute the Office of President of the United States, and will to the best of my Ability, preserve, protect and defend the Constitution of the United States." That mandate to "protect and defend" was a broad-based, powerful legal tool enabling the president to justify serious security measures during wartime.

Another tool at his disposal was suspension of the writ of habeas corpus. Latin for "have the body," the writ of habeas corpus was typically filed by an incarcerated person's attorney as a way of compelling the government to prove it possessed sufficient evidence to make an arrest and was considered to be one of the most fundamental safeguards of a citizen's civil liberties against a government that might use its police and military powers to jail people and throw away the key.[8]

Most authorities admitted that circumstances might arise, particularly in wartime, when suspension of the writ was necessary to maintain national security. The Founding Fathers gave the federal government explicit consent to suspend the writ in Article I, Section 9, but only "when in Cases of Rebellion or Invasion the public safety may require it." They were realists and understood that sometimes strong (if limited) application of government power was necessary. But as with everything else related to the Constitution and war, no one knew exactly how strong or how limited, particularly in the area of habeas corpus; the writ had never been suspended by the federal government.[9]

What must have been striking to Lincoln in the early days of his presidency was how little any of this had to do with his Declaration-centered constitutionalism. He had come of age as an American politician of substance in the 1850s by formulating a constitutional doctrine designed to eventually rid the nation of slavery. While slavery would eventually reassert itself as a crucial wartime constitutional issue, during the first months of his presidency, it seemed more of a secondary issue, taking a backseat to the more elemental problem of national survival. America's "peculiar institution" might no longer be an American problem, because there was a very real chance that America itself would cease to exist.

On December 20, 1860, South Carolina began the march towards civil war when its state legislature ratified with unanimous vote an ordinance of secession. Six other Southern states followed suit, and by February they had created a new constitution and government, styled the Confederate States of America, with a constitution and a government patterned on a longstanding Southern tradition of protecting slavery, preserving white supremacy, and limiting national government power—in many ways the antithesis of everything Lincoln valued. Standing before a cheering crowd in front of the statehouse in Montgomery, Alabama, after he took the oath of office, Jefferson Davis exulted, "it is joyous in perilous times to look around upon a people united in heart, who are animated and actuated by one and the same purpose and high resolve, with whom the sacrifices to be made are not weighed in the balance against honor, right, liberty and equality."[10]

The North, on the other hand, seemed confused, distracted, and uncertain. This sense of malaise was partly due to a peculiar circumstance of the American political system. Presidential elections are held in November, but the victor does not take office until several months later. Normally this time lag is of no consequence. The outgoing president keeps the seat warm until the new president settles in, smoothly and seamlessly. But in the winter of 1860, the outgoing president was James Buchanan, and that made all the difference.

Buchanan was a genial sort who hailed from Pennsylvania but had many Southern friends; the perfect president when elected in 1856 to hold a quavering America together.[11] Four years later, however, with the nation in the throes of disunion and impending civil war, Buchanan's mellow, fence-sitting persona was more a handicap than a help. In the weeks after Lincoln's election, the seceding states called special sessions, voted themselves out of the Union, and seized federal property within their borders, including military installations and weapons that would someday soon be used to kill US soldiers. In nearly every case, military commanders handed over their equipment without protest, because they had no orders from Buchanan to do otherwise. The North was embarrassed. When on January 4 Buchanan called for a day of fasting and prayer, a New York newspaper scoffed that "God helps those who help themselves. There are no records of miracles on behalf of the sluggard."[12]

As president-elect, Lincoln could do nothing, because he had not yet taken the oath of office. "Please present my respects to [army general Winfield Scott]," he wrote to an ally in December, "and tell him, confidentially, I shall be obliged to him to be as well prepared as he can to either *hold*, or *retake*, the forts, as the case may require, at, and after the inauguration." Lincoln had the will to act, but not the power. Buchanan possessed the power to act, but not the will.[13]

Buchanan was not a coward or a fool. Nor was he (as some at the time charged) a closet Confederate sympathizer. An experienced and respected statesman, one-time cabinet member, and diplomat, he should have been able to lead, in some capacity. But he could not.

Why? Because Buchanan was hamstrung by his constitutionalism. The first question any president must ask before contemplating action is: What does the Constitution allow me to do? Buchanan's answer was alarming: hardly anything at all. He was a lifelong strict constructionist and advocate of limited federal authority. In his annual State of the Union address, delivered two weeks before South Carolina's formal break with the Union, Buchanan did denounce the doctrine of secession, declaring the notion "that the Federal Government is a mere voluntary association of States, to be dissolved at pleasure by any one of the contracting parties," turning the Union into a mere "rope of sand, to be penetrated and dissolved by the first adverse wave of public opinion in any of the States." He also stated his belief that the Union was perpetual and permanent, run by "a great and powerful Government, invested with all the attributes of sovereignty. . . . Its framers never intended to implant in its bosom the seeds of its own destruction, nor were they at its creation guilty of the absurdity of providing for its own dissolution."

So far, so good. But then Buchanan rendered his constitutional lecture toothless by declaring he had no power to enforce his own views. Acknowledging that he was bound by oath to "to take care that the laws be faithfully executed," Buchanan meekly confessed that "the performance of this duty, in whole or in part, has been rendered impracticable by events over which he could have exercised no control." "In fact," he said, "the whole machinery of the Federal Government necessary for the distribution of remedial justice among the people [in South Carolina] has been demolished, and it would be difficult, if not impossible, to replace it." So he would just hope the people of South Carolina (along with the rest of the lower South) would listen to reason and remain in the Union. Otherwise? The president responded with a rhetorical shrug. "The Executive has no authority to decide what shall be the relations between the Federal Government and South Carolina. He has been invested with no such discretion."[14]

This abdication of power made Buchanan something of a hero in the South (along with his having devoted the early part of his address to berating abolitionists for having provoked the sectional crisis). But it satisfied almost no one in the North. Senator John P. Hale of New Hampshire sarcastically restated Buchanan's argument thus: "South Carolina has just cause for seceding from the Union; that is the first proposition. The second is, she has no right to secede. The third is, we have no right to prevent her from seceding." Hale spoke for the sentiments of many when he added that, to his mind, Buchanan had "failed to look the thing in the face. He has acted like the ostrich, which hides her head, and thereby thinks to escape danger."[15]

Buchanan became a convenient scapegoat for the secession catas-trophe, and in many ways deservedly so. But the North's paralysis extended beyond the presidency. Congress was as confused and tepid as Buchanan, failing to pass appropriations bills that might have given the president the means necessary to defend what was left of federal property in the South: not just Fort Sumter in Charleston, but several other minor military installations in Florida and elsewhere. To those who criticized him for his torpor, Buchanan correctly replied that Congress seemed no more inclined to do anything.[16]

Some did try to step into the breach and offer last-ditch solu-tions. Senator John Crittenden of Kentucky—whose state lay in the path of the tornado, should war come—led a committee that introduced a series of resolutions on December 18 designed to bring the South peacefully back into the Union. Their solution was simple: give Southerners nearly everything they want, and then make the victory so permanent they would never again feel threatened by the specter of losing their slaves. They proposed reestablishing the Missouri Compromise line, guaranteeing slavery's existence in the western territories south of the 36°30' line, and prohibiting Congress from ever interfering thereafter. Congress could not abolish slavery at military posts, it could not get rid of slavery in the District of Columbia without prior consent of the district's citizens (and even then, it had to compensate the owners), it could not interfere with the interstate slave trade, and it was required to reimburse slave owners for the expenses they incurred in recapturing slaves who ran away to the North. If any antislavery Northerners interfered, the federal government could "sue the county in which said violence, intimida-tion, or rescue was committed, and to recover from it, with interest and damages, the amount paid by them for said fugitive slave."

The committee proposed its resolutions as a series of constitutional amendments—the best way to assure that a policy was beyond revo-cation, given the difficulties involved in changing the Constitution's text. But some in Congress were spooked so badly that even this was not enough. They invented a new tool, virtually unknown to Ameri-can constitutionalism before or since: the unamendable amendment. All those proslavery changes would be capped off with a provision that "no future amendment of the Constitution shall affect the five preceding articles."[17]

It was a remarkable proposition, one that would have set the institution of human bondage beyond the normal political machinery of the Constitution and into some nether world where it could never be addressed or rectified on a national level. Of all the many policies, laws, and institutions in what was becoming a vast and growing country, slavery would become the sole subject beyond deliberation: the crazy aunt locked away in the basement, of whom no one could speak. The Union might subsequently be preserved and war averted, but at a high cost to a nation whose democracy was predicated on the notion that all subjects were fit for debate.[18]

Here was one sort of constitutional vision given by Buchanan and Crittenden's committee: a watered-down states' rights vision of the Constitution, whereby the federal government was severely restricted from taking any vigorous action, unless in defense of slavery. Hale's assessment of Buchanan as an "ostrich" was a bit harsh, but it would be fair to characterize the entire Buchanan/Crittenden axis of constitutional thought as running scared: scared of the South's political power, and of possible disunion and civil war.

And president-elect Abraham Lincoln—what constitutional vision did the new president-elect represent?

His inaugural address would be his first serious, deliberate speech concerning secession. He did deliver impromptu talks at train stations and from hotel balconies while traveling from Springfield to Washington, DC. But he was circumspect almost to a fault, refusing to offer any extended analysis of the crisis for fear his words would be misconstrued and only make matters worse.[19] Arriving in Philadelphia, Lincoln took part in a flag-raising ceremony at Independence Hall, one with a new star representing Kansas's recent admission into the Union as a free state. The moment was emotional, and Lincoln spoke with passion. "All the political sentiments I entertain have been drawn, so far as I have been able to draw them, from the sentiments which originated, and were given to the world from this hall in which we stand," he told the crowd. "I have never had a feeling politically that did not spring from the sentiments embodied in the Declaration of Independence." Pointing out that the Declaration embodied the principle that "in due time the weights should be lifted from the shoulders of all men, and that *all* should have an equal chance," Lincoln stated; "if this country cannot be saved without giving up that principle . . ." he paused; "I was about to say I would rather be assassinated on this spot than to surrender it."[20]

In his inaugural address Lincoln did offer some cautious support to the Crittenden committee's efforts at compromise. "I can not be ignorant of the fact that many worthy, and patriotic citizens are desirous of having the national constitution amended," he noted, and "while I make no recommendation of amendments, I fully recognize the rightful authority of the people over the whole subject . . . and I should, under existing circumstances, favor, rather than oppose, a fair oppertunity [*sic*] being afforded the people to act upon it."

It was hard to say whether this was an endorsement of the Crittenden efforts or not (which was probably just the effect Lincoln sought). At any event, Lincoln did not see the need for further guarantees to mollify white Southerners, as they had nothing to fear from him or other Republicans. "All profess to be content in the Union, if all constitutional rights can be maintained," he pointed out. "Is it true, then, that any right, plainly written in the Constitution, has been denied [to Southerners]? I think not. . . . [T]hink, if you can, of a single instance in which a plainly written provision of the Constitution has ever been denied."

That said, Lincoln would not concede that slaveholders' constitutional guarantees to have their slaves protected in the South, and to have fugitive slaves returned to them, meant that the federal government had no business at all in restricting slavery's growth, or undertaking policies that would someday promote slavery's eventual demise. Lincoln here displayed his Hamiltonian, broad constructionist instincts, arguing that the Constitution's silence on such subjects as slavery's expansion left open the possibility that Congress could do what Republicans wanted it to do: limit slavery's growth. "No organic law can ever be framed with a provision specifically applicable to every question which may occur in practical administration," he argued, and "no foresight can anticipate, nor any document of reasonable length contain express provisions for all possible questions. . . . *May* Congress prohibit slavery in the territories? The Constitution does not expressly say. *Must* Congress protect slavery in the territories? The Constitution does not expressly say."

Since there was no specific constitutional language on these subjects, democracy must decide; and Americans had decided. They put Lincoln in the White House knowing he would do whatever he could to keep slavery contained in the South. If Southerners had a problem with this, then they would have ample opportunity to make their case to the rest of the nation and vote him out of office. "By the frame of the government under which we live, [Americans] have wisely given their public servants but little power for mischief," he assured Southerners, "and have, with equal wisdom, provided for the return of that little to their own hands at very short intervals." In the meantime, Southern rights as a legitimate minority were fully protected by the Constitution.

But whatever Southerners' fears, secession was certainly not the answer. If American constitutionalism provided order and stability to American lives, then secession was the exact opposite; it was "the essence of anarchy." "A majority, held in restraint by constitutional checks, and limitations, and always changing easily, with deliberate changes of popular opinions and sentiments, is the only true sovereign of a free people," Lincoln argued. "Whoever rejects it, does, of necessity, fly to anarchy or to despotism. Unanimity is impossible; the rule of a minority, as a permanent arrangement, is wholly inadmissable; so that, rejecting the majority principle, anarchy, or despotism in some form, is all that is left."

Lincoln here offered a negative critique of secession as a political and practical act. But he also took issue with secession on positive grounds, arguing not just that secession was bad, but also that the national community, the Union, was good. In doing so, he introduced what would become the bedrock feature of his wartime constitutionalism: Lincoln's unshakeable, core belief in a permanent, inviolate American national community.

He told his inauguration audience that the Union was by definition unbreakable. "I hold, that in contemplation of universal law, and of the Constitution, the Union of these States is perpetual." Part of this was for Lincoln simply a matter of logic and basic political science. "No government proper, ever had a provision in its organic law for its own termination," he argued. "Perpetuity is implied, if not expressed, in the fundamental law of all national governments."

History as well as logic established the fact of a permanent American Union. "We the people" was not just pretty language that introduced the American Constitution: It signified a culmination of nationalizing forces that had been gathering long before 1787. "The Union is much older than the Constitution," Lincoln believed. "It was formed in fact, by the Articles of Association in 1774. It was matured and continued by the Declaration of Independence in 1776. It was further matured and the faith of all the then thirteen States expressly plighted and engaged that it should be perpetual, by the Articles of Confederation in 1778. And finally, in 1787, one of the declared objects for ordaining and establishing the Constitution, was "*to form a more perfect union.*"

Here was Lincoln the historian, a man who had been reading of the Revolutionary era and its works since he was a boy, making a sophisticated and mature historical argument: namely, that the Union was a thing born of a long-percolating process, older than not only the Constitution, but even Lincoln's beloved Declaration of Independence. If the Constitution was the silver frame and the Declaration the golden apple, then the Union, the American historical community as a whole, was something deeper and more profound than either.

This notion of a historically grounded, almost mystical American nation was the key difference between Lincoln's constitutionalism and that of the Confederacy. Following their Calhounian roots, the Confederacy's founders went out of their way to avoid suggesting that there was any such thing as a single Confederate national community. To them, the nexus of community was local and went no further than a state's boundaries. American constitutionalism, properly understood, was only a marriage of convenience between constituent states, and no more. The various states in 1787 acted "as distinct and sovereign political communities," Jefferson Davis wrote in his interpretation of the Founding era. "The monstrous fiction that they acted as one people 'in their aggregate capacity' has not an atom of fact to serve as a basis."[21]

That "monstrous fiction" was the very foundation upon which Lincoln chose to base his presidency; and unlike his predecessor, Lincoln found the power necessary to defend the nation against secession. "I therefore consider that, in view of the Constitution and the laws, the Union is unbroken; and, to the extent of my ability, I shall take care, as the Constitution itself expressly enjoins upon me, that the laws of the Union be faithfully executed in all the States," he stated. "Doing this I deem to be only a simple duty on my part; and I shall perform it, so far as practicable, unless my rightful masters, the American people, shall withhold the requisite means, or, in some authoritative manner, direct the contrary."

Buchanan had served up a spirited defense of the Union, to be sure, but he had never suggested that its defense carried such legal and moral weight. Lincoln did; and there were interesting implications in what he said.

Since the nation's founding, Americans had long debated whether or not there was a higher law than the Constitution itself. Did there exist an extralegal moral code that superseded the nation's founding document—the Sermon on the Mount, for example, or the Golden Rule, or perhaps some Lockean, Enlightenment notion of a "natural law" inherent in the human condition?[22]

By Lincoln's time, many Americans associated higher law arguments with abolitionism, because abolitionists were given to arguing that the will of God, the dictates of human decency, or some other higher moral standard than the Constitution—which after all did provide slavery legal protection—offered the necessary moral foundation for fighting slavery. When abolitionist activists broke the law to aid runaway slaves, for example, they justified their actions by arguing that they had a duty to the "higher law" of God that frowned upon human bondage and its enforcement. "Let [slaveholders] tell us distinctly, in plain Saxon English, what they believe in respect to the righteousness or unrighteousness of capturing men and sending them back to the bondage of Slavery," declared one abolitionist minister in an 1850 sermon titled *The Law-Abiding Conscience and Higher Law Conscience.* "We concede that it is constitutional, while we believe it to be morally wrong."[23]

This bothered many Americans, however, because it was so ambiguous as to seem dangerous: Allow policies based on wispy and subjective ideals like the "will of God," or whatever, and pretty soon the government could justify all sorts of intrusions and tyrannies in the name of enforcing a "higher law." Southerners bristled at the mere suggestion of a moral code that superseded the Constitution, and even most moderate Northerners thought the whole idea was disturbing. Politicians bucked this trend at their peril. William Seward—who for all his intelligence and skill could be surprisingly tone deaf—had gotten himself into trouble in a Senate speech during which he argued that slavery could be excluded from the western territories because "there is a higher law than the Constitution, which regulates our authority. . . . [It is] the common heritage of mankind, bestowed upon them by the Creator of the universe."[24]

That "higher law" reference had a great deal to do with Seward's loss to Lincoln for the Republican nomination in 1860, because it made him look like an abolitionist hothead. Lincoln was too shrewd a politician to echo Seward's mistake by invoking something as vague and threatening as an extraconstitutional "higher law."[25] He privately believed that slavery was very much a violation of fundamental human morality—"if slavery is not wrong, then nothing is wrong"—universal ideas of fairness, and God's will. But he needed something more concrete and tangible upon which to fasten his antislavery principles, lest he torpedo his own political prospects and those of his party by inviting association with radical abolitionists. So in the 1850s, he turned to the Declaration of Independence: the apple of gold for which the Constitution's silver frame was made. This served his purposes well during that time, connecting his antislavery goals to a tangible and respected Revolutionary-era document—one written by a Southerner, no less.

As secession and civil war loomed over his presidency, Lincoln certainly still revered the Declaration, but he had begun the process of quietly pushing it into the background. That speech before

Independence Hall would be the last time he placed such a heavy emphasis on the Declaration. In fact, it would be one of the last times he mentioned the document at all.

He never said exactly why; there were probably several reasons. The Declaration was fundamentally a justification of separation from the mother country of Great Britain, and this was uneasily close to secession. The cautious politician in Lincoln may also have been wary of invoking the Declaration's "all men are created equal" mantra. If he mentioned the Declaration's promise of equality for all, he risked setting off a whole new round of fears in the South concerning just what he intended to do about slavery. Or he may have thought that the Declaration was unequal to the task of war: Did it really speak to the difficult legal and constitutional questions he now confronted concerning wartime administration, separation of powers, and national security?

However much Lincoln might have insisted he "never had a feeling politically" that did not spring from the Declaration of Independence, in reality the Declaration was for Lincoln a tool, one that was inadequate to the task of defining Lincoln's approach to the harsh new realities of the war. He needed something else, some other source of inspiration and guidance that he could use to inspire both himself and others, and could act as something akin to a higher law that was both detached from and related to the Constitution.

He found it in the idea of the Union, which he now, on the very day of his inauguration, placed at the forefront of his presidency and his constitutional interpretation of the crisis. To be sure, his use of the Union differed somewhat from that of the abolitionists of the 1850s. They argued that there was a conflict between a higher moral law and the Constitution; Lincoln suggested that there was an essential harmony between his "higher law"—the Union—and the Constitution, that they in fact complemented one another. But Lincoln's proposal of a Union as separate from and older than the Constitution served the same general purpose.

The concept of the Union solved problems for him, in much the same way that the Declaration solved the difficulties he encountered in trying to articulate a viable antislavery constitutionalism during the 1850s. The Union allowed him to circumnavigate the Calhounian, state sovereignty strain of American thought, popular among some Northerners as well as Southerners, which held that the Union was transient and under some circumstances breakable. It also gave his arguments significant force, more so than anything James Buchanan and others of his ilk could muster. Whereas before the war Lincoln's chief task was articulating a constitutional vision that avoided the amoral acquiescence to slavery preferred by people like Stephen Douglas, now he had to find a constitutional vision that was adequate to the task of fighting a long, hard civil war.

This was not easy. That Abraham Lincoln, the onetime "little Illinois lawyer" and supposed frontier hick could, with intellectual sophistication and nimble flexibility, shift his thought to such a new, different, and (as events would prove) effective constitutionalism spoke well of his capacity to meet the difficult new circumstances that confronted the nation. He would make mistakes, to be sure. But there was steel in the man, and in his newfound Union-centered constitutionalism.

THE WAR, CIVIL LIBERTIES,

AND *EX PARTE MERRYMAN*

R oger Taney's "agitation" lasted long after inauguration day. Speculation swirled concerning his loyalties. There were those who interpreted his proslavery extremism—so evident in the *Dred Scott* case—and intense dislike of the Republican Party as evidence of closet Confederate sympathies. But Taney was actually not a secessionist; rather, his constitutional position on the issue looked much like President Buchanan's. Taney believed the white South had received more than enough provocation at the hands of the abolitionists, but he argued against the propriety and the constitutionality of secession. That said, he also (like Buchanan) held a strict constructionist's carefully proscribed view of federal authority, and he shrank from using federal power to coerce the Southern states back into the Union. Taney wrote former president Franklin Pierce that he hoped "calmer and more sober thoughts" would prevent the secession crisis from destroying the country. But if this happened, the chief justice believed, then "peaceful separation" was better than "a civil war with all its horrors."[1]

The old man suffered from the infirmities afflicting a man in his eighties, and there were periodic rumors around Washington that he might at any moment retire, or die. But he showed no inclination to do either. Taney remained on the bench, a dour critic of the Lincoln administration and the war, like a dark cloud hovering just over the horizon. "At my advanced age, I can hardly hope to see the end of the evil times into which we have fallen," the justice dejectedly wrote to a friend. Taney was decidedly of the opinion that the man in the White House was primarily responsible for those evil times.[2]

Lincoln worked under many dark clouds during the spring and summer of 1861. After Confederate authorities fired upon the Union garrison at Fort Sumter in Charleston harbor, Lincoln responded with a call for seventy-five thousand volunteers from the loyal states to put down the rebellion, which he described as "combinations too powerful to be suppressed by the ordinary course of judicial proceedings, or by the powers vested in the Marshals by law." His language made the war sound more like a law enforcement matter than a conventional war against a conventional foe, and in fact he justified his response to the rebellion by citing Article II, Section 3's charge that the president ensure the laws of the land are "faithfully executed."[3]

The response among the North's young men to Lincoln's call was enthusiastic, as thousands volunteered to serve in the Union army. But another immediate consequence of Lincoln's call for volunteers was decidedly negative: four more slaveholding states—Arkansas, Tennessee, North Carolina, and (the grand prize) Virginia—left the Union and joined the Confederacy. Senator James Mason of Virginia spoke for many when he wrote to a local newspaper that, if Virginia remained in the Union, the state must face the awful prospect that, "under orders of the [federal] Government, [Virginia must] turn her arms against her Southern sisters."[4]

Losing these states was a major setback for Lincoln; and still larger disasters loomed. Missouri, Kentucky, and Maryland, the major "Border States," also teetered on the brink of secession. Lincoln faced a serious problem here, and he knew it. "I think to lose Kentucky is nearly the same as to lose the whole game," he believed. "Kentucky gone, we can not hold Missouri, nor, as I think, Maryland. These all against us, and the job on our hands is too large for us. We would as well consent to separation at once, including the surrender of this capitol."[5]

But events could also swing the other way in those confused early days of the war. Many Southerners weren't enamored of secession or the Confederacy, and while most kept quiet, some did not. The mountainous western region of Virginia was especially vocal in its opposition to a Confederate future. Loyalty to the Confederacy generally mirrored loyalty to slavery, and western Virginia never possessed many slaves.[6]

Unlike opponents of secession in other Southern states, western Virginia's Unionists quickly organized themselves and led opposition to a statewide secession referendum. When they were unable to prevent Virginia's separation from the Union, they called a convention that created a new Unionist state government and appointed pro-Lincoln lawyer and activist Francis H. Pierpont as their new governor. Pierpont promptly contacted Lincoln and asked for the president's aid.[7]

Western Virginia's Unionists believed they might need to separate from Virginia entirely and form a new state, creating what they at first called "New Virginia."[8] There was, however, a thorny constitutional problem. Article IV, Section 3 contains a little noticed rule that "no new States shall be formed or erected within the Jurisdiction of any other State . . . without the Consent of the Legislatures of the States concerned as well as of the Congress." As with so much else in the Constitution, the Framers had good reasons for including this rule; no one wanted to see states carving away parts of other states without their consent, creating all manner of confusion and controversy. But again, as with so much else in the Constitution, the Framers had not foreseen the peculiar circumstances created by a civil war, with one part of a state remaining loyal to the Union and another part not. [9]

To conform to the letter of the Constitution, western Virginia's bid for separation could occur only with the approval of the Confederate state legislature in Richmond, which was hardly likely. West Virginia's Unionist legislature tried to get around this by assuming the title "restored Government of Virginia," as if it were the governing body for the entire state. It then gave itself permission to secede from Virginia; once it did so, the new "state" of West Virginia quickly ratified a constitution and applied for admission to the Union.

Strictly speaking, this was Congress's mess more than the president's, since the Constitution gives Congress authority over the procedures by which states are admitted into the Union. But Lincoln would have had to either sign or veto the bill that Congress eventually passed for West Virginia's admission. The president was worried enough about the legality of the whole affair that he took the relatively rare step of soliciting written opinions from each cabinet member concerning the bill's constitutionality. His cabinet was worried, too: Half supported the bill; the other half were opposed.[10]

Lincoln was not about to turn his back on the West Virginians, and half a cabinet was better than no support at all. He signed the bill and forwarded a message to Congress explaining why. He defended the notion that the true legislature of "Virginia" had given permission for the split, arguing that the "restored Government of Virginia" and its legislature did actually represent the will of Virginia's voters—or at least, those who chose to vote for a Unionist government. If secessionist-minded Virginians chose not to participate in this election process, so be it. "It is a universal practice in the popular elections in all these states, to give no legal consideration whatever to those who do not choose to vote," Lincoln argued, "as against the effect of the votes of those, who do choose to vote. Hence it is not the qualified voters, but the qualified voters, *who choose to vote*, that constitute the political power of the state. Much less than to non-voters, should any consideration be given to those who did not vote, *in this case*: because it is also matter of outside knowledge, that they were not merely neglectful of their rights under, and duty to, this government, but were also engaged in open rebellion against it."

This argument could seem like little more than a particularly foggy (and self-serving) species of constitutional legerdemain, so Lincoln decided it also would be wise to come clean about the practical reasons for his actions. He pointed out that West Virginia's admission into the Union was frankly "expedient," and a boon to the Union's cause—and such practical considerations mattered a great deal, perhaps more than crossing every *t* and dotting every *i* in the Constitution. "More than on anything else, [the question] depends on whether the admission or rejection of the new state would under all the circumstances tend the more strongly to the restoration of the national authority throughout the Union," Lincoln argued. "That which helps most in this direction is the most expedient at this time." Moreover, Lincoln believed the rest of the country owed something to West Virginia's Unionists. "We can scarcely dispense with the aid of West-Virginia in this struggle," he pointed out; "her brave and good men regard her admission into the Union as a matter of life and death. They have been true to the Union under very severe trials. We have so acted as to justify their hopes; and we can not fully retain their confidence, and co-operation, if we seem to break faith with them."[11]

The West Virginia problem illustrates a basic constitutional question that confronted Lincoln from the very beginning of the war: a question of what we might call the Constitution's elasticity.

In his inaugural address, Lincoln identified an overarching principle, the Union, around which to arrange his wartime constitutionalism. He now had the Union as his higher law, his "apple of gold," a high ideal of American community with which he rallied his fellow Americans when they needed to be reminded of why they were fighting and dying. The Union justified the war and provided the best available means by which Lincoln could instigate the battle hymn of the republic.

But once that martial music started, and Lincoln embarked the country on the terrible and uncertain project of civil war, would he have tools at his disposal to see the thing through? This was more than a matter of bombs and bullets; he needed legal tools, as well, for as the defender of the Union and the Constitution, he was the voice of law and order. In combating the anarchy of secession, Lincoln could not become himself the voice of anarchy. In his time of war, the laws could not fall silent. Lincoln *was* the law.

But law and order were not such simple matters, not in that day and age. Lincoln needed a variety of legal tools, some never before tried or tested. He also needed the will and the means to take action when the existing laws were silent or inadequate to the exigencies of the war. To find the legal means necessary for defending his high end of the Union, Lincoln needed a Constitution that was adjustable to the rapidly changing circumstances of a massive civil war. He needed elasticity.

Those Americans who approached the war from the perspective of a James Buchanan or a Roger Taney saw the Constitution as a strong but brittle instrument. Bend its words too far by reading into their meaning powers never intended by the Framers, and their Constitution would break. It was an admirable quality, this dogged tenacity with which they clung to strict constructionist, limited government principles, come what may. Their concerns about tyranny and runaway government authority were valid. But there was also a cure-the-disease-by-killing-the-patient dimension to their principles. Buchanan and Taney would have seen the nation dissolve and its Constitution shattered via a "peaceful separation," rather than violate their narrow interpretation of Constitutional language.

Lincoln could ill-afford such a perspective. He faced a fluid and rapidly evolving situation, calling for constant adaptability and creative thinking. Sometimes the Constitution provided clear, unambiguous guidance—but more often not. More often there were gray areas, empty spaces between the Constitution's words that needed to be filled, lest the enterprise of American democracy fall to pieces. Lincoln famously saw the war as the ultimate test of that democracy, and he saw its ruin in the success of the Confederacy, secession, and separation. So he acted; and his actions often bent and flexed the law and the Constitution to fit the odd new shape of the war.

His most difficult problem early in the war was simply identifying the enemy. This was particularly true in Maryland, where secessionist sympathies ran very high. If that state joined the Confederacy, Lincoln would have to abandon Washington, DC, a blow from which the Union cause might not recover. In the spring of 1861, this appeared a distinct possibility. The press reported pro-Confederate spies and saboteurs roaming the Maryland countryside, drumming up recruits for the Rebel army, gathering information about Union troop movements to pass along to the Confederacy, and laying plans for every manner of sabotage—blowing up bridges, cutting telegraph wires, blocking railroads, almost any act of material destruction that was likely to aid the Confederate cause. Throughout April and into May, increasingly alarming rumors and reports reached Lincoln's desk that Maryland was teetering on the very brink of secession and lawless pandemonium. "For Gods [*sic*] sake, dont put your trust in the

Union men of Maryland," a citizen named Oliver Dyer telegraphed Lincoln on May 2. "As soon as it will be safe for them to rush to the standard of Jeff. Davis they will do so."[12]

Worse still, Lincoln was told that if the state legislature convened, its members could very well vote Maryland out of the Union. "The passage of that ordnance will be the signal for disunion forces to enter Maryland," warned Lincoln's secretary of the treasury, Salmon Chase; "it will give a color of law and regularity to rebellion and thereby triple its strength." A fair number—perhaps a majority—of the legislators were at least open to the possibility, and people throughout Maryland debated the legality and the propriety of either a legislative vote on the issue, or the calling of a statewide meeting. Governor Thomas Hicks, a former Democrat and outspoken critic of abolitionism, called a special session of the legislature to debate these very issues. No one knew where this might lead.[13]

Lincoln's most immediate and obvious option was to send in the army, declare martial law, and suspend the writ of habeas corpus. "A word to the brave old commanding General [Scott] will do the work of prevention," Chase urged the president, "and you alone can give the word."[14] But this posed a problem of timing.

The Constitution's authorization for the federal government to suspend the writ appears in a brief sentence in Article I, Section 9: "The Privilege of the Writ of Habeas Corpus shall not be suspended, unless when in Cases of Rebellion or Invasion the Public Safety may require it." Section 9 lists limitations on Congress's powers, so it was widely assumed by legal authorities in Lincoln's day that suspension of habeas corpus required prior congressional approval.[15]

Unfortunately, in the spring of 1861, Congress was out of town. Lincoln called it back into special session, but by the time Congress reassembled, Maryland might very well have already separated from the Union, or at the very least, her many pro-Confederate citizens might be ready to wreak havoc on the Union's war preparations and efforts to defend the capital.

The president was a lawyer, with a keen understanding of legal language. He noted that the actual wording of the Constitution's habeas corpus provision was passive voice: It did not specify exactly who was responsible for suspending the writ. To Lincoln's mind, this offset its location in Article I, Section 9. The Framers may have intended prior congressional approval, or maybe not—the matter was ambiguous. And Lincoln was in a hurry.

He allowed the special session of the Maryland legislature to meet on April 26, despite urging from some of his more alarmed military commanders that it would be best to break up the session and arrest the legislators. Lincoln thought this was both impolitic and unnecessary. He was right; the Maryland assembly failed to either enact an ordinance of secession or call a special convention. Lincoln and his generals breathed a sigh of relief. But he also made it clear to General Scott that, had they voted for secession, he would have authorized army action, including suspension of the writ.[16]

While the danger of secession by the state legislature at least temporarily abated, rumors continued to surface of clandestine plots afoot in Maryland to sabotage the federal government's mobilization efforts by blocking the various routes army units were required to take through the state to reach Washington, DC. Troops were just barely beginning to trickle eastward, and army authorities feared they would be too small in number to defend the capital, or even the White House itself, from a determined Confederate attack. Surveying one of the few regiments he actually had on hand to defend Washington, a worried Lincoln remarked, "I begin to believe that there is no North."[17]

On April 27, Lincoln wrote a private letter to General Scott, authorizing him to suspend the writ as he saw fit, but within narrowly proscribed limitations. He restricted Scott's suspension powers only to those areas in and around the primary military lines of reinforcement between Philadelphia and Washington, DC. Lincoln was worried about getting troops quickly and safely into the capital; his targets were military saboteurs, not political opponents. "Suspending the writ of habeas corpus was not originally a political measure," notes historian Mark Neely in his careful examination of the subject, "and it would never become primarily political."[18]

Even so, Lincoln took a cautious approach. The letter to Scott was not an executive order or other public document. Few people in Maryland—even local judges—were aware of what Lincoln had done.[19] The president also shared some of the responsibility with General Scott. While he authorized the writ's suspension, Scott would do the actual suspending, and he, Scott, would decide exactly where and when this was to take place. It may also not have been lost on Lincoln that Scott was a Virginian. The writ would be suspended in a Southern state by another Southerner, perhaps softening somewhat the sectional animus of the measure.

With Lincoln's letter in hand, Scott and the army moved swiftly and began to arrest Marylanders suspected of supporting secession or the Confederate cause. "We are now surrounded with US troops to keep Maryland in the Union," wrote a distressed Baltimore servant to his employer in Paris, "and what things will come to, I cannot imagine."[20] On the whole, however, public reaction was muted. Again, few Marylanders were aware that the army now operated under suspension of the writ. After waiting a few days to gauge the response, Lincoln felt more confident. On May 10, he publicly authorized army authorities in Florida—where the Union still occupied some forts—to "remove from the vicinity of the United States fortresses all dangerous or suspected persons," and to suspend the writ when necessary.[21]

Like a person slowly growing accustomed to feeling his way around a dark room, Lincoln with each new step increased the scope of the suspensions and arrests. On July 2, he again wrote General Scott: "if, at any point, on or in the vicinity of any military line which is now, or which shall be used, between the City of New York and the City of Washington, you find resistance which renders it necessary to suspend the writ of Habeas Corpus for the Public Safety, you, personally, or through the Officer in command, at the point where resistance occurs, are authorized to suspend that writ."[22]

Lincoln was trying to find an acceptable middle ground between an overly restrictive application of the military's martial law powers and a grant of authority that might allow the army to arrest people without good cause. His suspension order was limited to military lines, and presumably any arrests had to be tied to securing these avenues of military movement and reinforcement. Still, "any military line" could plausibly be defined as any road, railroad, or waterway within the approximately two-hundred-mile distance between New York and Washington. "Vicinity" was also a fuzzy concept. Theoretically the army could suspend the writ along a large portion of the North's eastern seaboard, and in the name of a nebulously rendered "public safety." Lincoln did not give General Scott a blank check to arrest whomever he wished, but he did give the general and his soldiers wide leeway in making arrests and depriving prisoners of their habeas corpus privileges.

The process by which Lincoln arrived at this point was not linear or tidy. He was a new president encountering a dangerous situation in unique circumstances. He possessed no secret plan, no predetermined blueprint for enlarging his administration's authority or the army's enforcement powers. He was reacting to the daily (and on the whole quite credible) reports of Maryland disloyalty that reached his desk; and while he acted with a slowly increasing sense of confidence in his constitutional authority, he was sometimes merely reacting to the actions taken by others. Some soldiers had already begun to arrest people and hold them without recourse to their habeas corpus rights before Lincoln's authorization.[23]

By May, the writ's suspension was making national news, and public opinion was sharply divided. For some, Lincoln's actions were a welcome sign of long-delayed vigor and energy in putting the brakes on treason. "The privilege of the writ of Habeas Corpus is a privilege for the conservation of personal liberty in time of peace," noted one supporter; "in cases of rebellion or invasion, the personal liberty of thousands is threatened, and, therefore, the suspension of the privilege of the writ to an individual suspected as an enemy is in obedience to the right to liberty of many individuals and the safety of the public."[24]

Others, however, were shocked. "So far as the violation of the writ of habeas corpus in the State of Maryland was concerned, I refuse to give [Lincoln] my sanction for that act," declared a California politician; "I refuse it because that State has shown, by the return of her delegates [to the House of Representatives], her allegiance to the Government of the United States; and though there may be many citizens in her midst who sympathize with the disloyal spirit of the Southern States [and] though there may have been disgraceful mobs and riots in the city of Baltimore . . . I would not justify any officer in the suspension of that sacred privilege." Another critic condemned the antidemocratic aspects of allowing the president to suspend the writ on his own hook with no input from Congress, writing that "such trust of power to one man is antagonistic to all republican teachings. Let the Federal Government do all it can to secure success in the present awful crisis—but for the sake of what is infinitely more dear than Union—liberty—let all acts emanate from the proper department."[25]

As the North debated, the arrests continued. At two o'clock in the morning on May 25, federal soldiers entered the home of John Merryman, a thirty-seven-year-old farmer living in Cockeysville, Maryland, just outside of Baltimore. He was accused of numerous pro-Confederate activities, including obstruction of the mail and sabotage performed on railroad bridges with an eye towards preventing soldiers from reinforcing Washington, DC—the very behavior that Lincoln's order suspending the writ of habeas corpus was aimed at curtailing. He was also the drill master of a Confederate militia company and had been outspoken in his loyalty for the Confederate cause. Merryman was escorted to Fort McHenry on the outskirts of Baltimore and placed in a prison cell, under the custody of Union general George Cadwalader.[26]

Merryman was only one of dozens suspected of Confederate sympathies and caught up in the army's net of arrests. He was unique, however, in that he had a powerful ally: Supreme Court chief justice Roger Brooke Taney. Taney seized upon Merryman's predicament as a test case that he hoped would not only stop Lincoln's internal security measures in Maryland, but also undermine the legal and constitutional rationale for what Taney regarded as a misbegotten war.

To this day, Taney's actions regarding Merryman's case are hard to fathom. Why for example did he choose Merryman, among all the people arrested by military authorities in Maryland, as his chief vehicle for attacking the Lincoln administration? There was also the matter of jurisdiction: Under what authority did Taney hear Merryman's case? In those days, members of the US Supreme Court wore two hats, acting as both Supreme Court justices and federal circuit court judges. Taney traveled from Washington to Baltimore—where he sat as a federal circuit court judge—to adjudicate the Merryman case, and so it was thought by many people then and since that Taney issued his ruling as a federal circuit court judge, rather than his capacity as chief justice of the Supreme Court. Recently, a careful examination of the Merryman case by Mark Neely has convincingly established that Taney issued *Ex Parte Merryman* in his capacity as a Supreme Court justice, although Neely also suggests that Taney's legal rationale for reviewing Merryman's case as a Supreme Court justice was suspect.[27]

Whatever the ambiguities, Taney leapt into action on May 27. From his Fort McHenry jail cell, Merryman filed a writ of habeas corpus with Taney, who promptly granted the request; he ordered General Cadwalader to honor the habeas corpus petition. The general refused, citing Lincoln's permission to suspend the writ. Taney then dispatched a US marshal with orders to arrest Cadwalader "for his contempt in refusing to produce the body of John Merryman." The marshal was turned away at Fort McHenry's front gate.[28]

Taney now had an opportunity to expound upon what he believed to be both Lincoln's secrecy and his erroneous constitutionalism. "No official notice has been given to the courts of justice, or to the public, by proclamation or otherwise, that the President claimed this power, and had exercised it in the manner stated in the return," Taney noted. "And I certainly listened to it with some surprise, for I had supposed it to be one of those points of constitutional law upon which there is no difference of opinion, and that it was admitted on all hands that the privilege of the writ could not be suspended except by act of Congress." The president had no business doing so on his own, and Taney could find no constitutional language indicating otherwise. "If the high power over the liberty of the citizens now claimed was intended to be conferred on the President, it would undoubtedly be found in plain words in [Article I]," he argued, "but there is not a word in it that can furnish the slightest ground to justify the exercise of the power."[29]

Taney argued that even Congress should be carefully proscribed from abusing the power to suspend the writ, by way of a narrowly restricted reading of the habeas corpus clause. Sounding a classic strict constructionist's tone, he wrote that "the power of legislation granted by this latter clause is by its word carefully confined to the specific objects before enumerated. . . . [A]nd the great importance which the framers of the Constitution attached to the privilege of the writ of *habeas corpus*, to protect the liberty of the citizen, is proved by the fact that its suspension, except in cases of invasion and rebellion, is first in the list of prohibited powers; and even in these cases the power is denied and its exercise prohibited unless the public safety shall require it. It is true that in the cases mentioned Congress is of necessity the judge of whether the public safety does or does not require it; and its judgment is conclusive. But the introduction of these words is a standing admonition to the legislative body of the danger of suspending it and of the extreme caution they should exercise before they give the Government of the United States such power over the liberty of a citizen."[30]

But Taney was after more than just a libertarian reading of the government's internal security powers. Four years previously, he had used *Dred Scott* as a vehicle for critiquing the American antislavery movement and the Republican Party. Now, he turned his habeas corpus argument into an extensive examination of presidential power.

Despite having once been employed by Andrew Jackson as attorney general, Taney was not on the whole enamored of strong executive authority, even in peacetime.[31] The war and his inherent distrust of Lincoln and his party exacerbated these concerns, and in his review of the Constitution's executive powers, Taney went out of his way to restrict the presidency to the narrowest and most limited possible authority, to the point that he touched upon matters not immediately germane to either Merryman or the writ of habeas corpus. Taney focused on the circumstance of presidential elections, noting that "the short term for which [the president] is elected, and the narrow limits to which his power is confined, show the jealousy and apprehensions of future danger which the framers of the Constitution felt in relation to that department of the Government, and how carefully they withheld from it many of the powers belonging to the executive branch of the English Government which were considered as dangerous to the liberty of the subject." Taney also touched upon presidential appointment powers, in a similarly narrowed fashion. "His powers in relation to the civil duties and authority necessarily conferred on him are carefully restricted. . . . He cannot appoint the ordinary officers of Government, nor make a treaty with a foreign nation or Indian tribe without the advice and consent of the Senate, and cannot appoint even inferior officers unless he is authorized by an act of Congress to do so."[32]

Turning to the particular matter of the president's war-making power, Taney was likewise concerned far more with limitation than expansion. He only rather grudgingly admitted that a president's role as commander in chief was "necessary" and then proceeded to list at length all of the various ways that this necessary role was restricted by the Constitution. "No appropriation for the support of the army can be made by Congress for a longer term than two years, so that it is in the power of the succeeding House of Representatives to withhold the appropriation for its support, and thus disband it, if, in their judgment, the President used or designed to use it for improper purposes," he pointed out, "and although the militia, when in actual service, are under his command, yet the appointment of the officers is reserved to the States, as a security against the use of the military power for purposes dangerous to the liberties of the people, or the rights of the States."

Taney cared only about what the president could not do, should not do, and must be prevented from doing. Nowhere in *Ex Parte Merryman*—or anyplace else—did Taney mention the extraordinary dangers posed to the American community by secession and disunion. At no point did he hint that a president was bound by oath to resist the destruction of the nation and dissolution of the Constitution's democratic process. Taney's Constitution in *Ex Parte Merryman* is an instrument of restriction, limitation, and restraint—it binds rather than expands, and it flexes not at all to meet the unusual circumstances of civil war.

Therein lay the problem with Taney's constitutional vision in the *Merryman* case: It is myopic, the very soul of "cannot." Taney did make some valid points, and his concerns about presidential excess still resonate, even today.[33] He spoke truth—yes, the Framers did want to impose boundaries on executive authority, and yes, the Constitution does try to restrict the potential for presidential excess—but only a small part of the truth. The Framers also wanted and expected a degree of energy and vigor in the nation's chief executive, and they imposed upon the president along with limitations a series of positive duties, a requirement via his oath of office to take the necessary steps to guard the Constitution and the vision of republican government it represented.

Taney concluded his *Merryman* opinion with a dark warning about would happen should the country suffer Lincoln to continue on his course. "I can only say that if the authority which the Constitution has confided to the judiciary department and judicial officers may thus upon any pretext or under any circumstances be usurped by the military power at its discretion," he wrote, then "the people of the United States are no longer living under a Government of laws, but every citizen holds life, liberty, and property at the will and pleasure of the army officer in whose military district he may happen to be found."[34]

These were provocative words—probably deliberately so. The *Merryman* case attracted a great deal of attention, particularly in Baltimore, where a crowd of over two thousand people gathered outside Taney's courtroom to hear what the judge would say when General Cadwalader failed to appear. Taney likely wanted a showdown with Lincoln, hoping that a public fracas with the president would arouse popular opinion on his side. Lincoln was after all a minority president, elected by less than half the American people. He was new on the job, and he had already attracted his fair share of critics. Taney, on the other hand, commanded the majesty and tradition of the United States Supreme Court and the federal judiciary. Plenty of people esteemed the men in the black robes, to such a high degree that Taney could reasonably expect to prevail in a political showdown with the president. Perhaps Lincoln would back off from some of his more aggressive policies, or even be forced by popular opinion to curtail the war itself. With more than a touch of ego, Taney seemed to believe he was a last bulwark against runaway tyranny. "I am an old man, a very old man, but perhaps I was preserved for this occasion," he remarked to Baltimore's mayor.[35]

But Lincoln would not rise to Taney's bait. In July, Congress finally convened its special session, and Lincoln composed a lengthy message to bring them up to date on the war effort. He did not mention Merryman or Taney by name, instead obliquely referring to the fact that his habeas corpus policies "are questioned; and the attention of the country has been called to the proposition that one who is sworn to 'take care that the laws be faithfully executed' should not himself violate them." Lincoln conceded no violation, arguing that the Constitution did not exactly specify who was responsible for suspending the writ during times of national emergency. "The provision [for suspending the writ] was plainly made for a dangerous emergency," Lincoln noted, and "it cannot be believed the framers of the instrument intended, that in every case, the danger should run its course, until Congress could be called together; the very assembling of which might be prevented, as was intended in this case, by the rebellion."

Even if one were to concede the point that the Framers wanted Congress to suspend the writ, Lincoln argued that there was still a significant case to be made for his policy on the grounds of pragmatic common sense. "Are all the laws, *but one*, to go unexecuted, and the government itself go to pieces, lest that one be violated?" he asked. "Even in such a case, would not the official oath be broken, if the government should be overthrown, when it was believed that disregarding the single law, would tend to preserve it?"[36]

Here was a case study in Lincoln's particular style of presidential leadership. As with the West Virginia issue, Lincoln could construct a viable lawyerly argument that his policies passed constitutional muster, and yet he also simultaneously pointed out that, in those extraordinary times, practical considerations were paramount. The North needed to win the war; Lincoln needed the constitutional wherewithal to make this happen.

To do so, he avoided an open confrontation with critics like Roger Taney, defending his policies while avoiding a direct, possibly disastrous rupture. There are shades of Lincoln's lawyerly past here, as he had learned a long time ago in all those Illinois courtrooms that open confrontation was generally a bad idea. Calling Taney out—and by association the US Supreme Court—would only harden opposition to his leadership.

Instead, he offered only an indirect criticism of Taney; and he worked behind the scenes, quietly utilizing the legal and political tools at his disposal. His Republican allies in Congress gave him most of what he wished, retroactively endorsing all his actions taken in their absence—everything, that is, except his suspension of the writ of habeas corpus (they eventually ratified even that controversial decision, passing the Habeas Corpus Act of 1863). Lincoln marshaled his legal forces, asking his attorney general, Edward Bates, to prepare a written argument supporting the constitutionality of the writ suspension. He also solicited a pamphlet from Maryland lawyer and jurist Reverdy Johnson to the same effect. This was a political coup for Lincoln, since Johnson was a conservative Democrat and former colleague of Taney.[37]

The result was that, in the end, *Ex Parte Merryman* exercised little direct impact on the war, or on the way the Lincoln administration dealt with civil liberties. Congress's endorsement of Lincoln's actions greatly diluted its impact. *Merryman* did become a rallying point for hardened critics of the Lincoln administration—but Lincoln harbored little hope of winning their support anyway. What did matter, politically speaking, was the support of moderates and conservatives like Reverdy Johnson, who seem to have accepted what Lincoln had done.

As it turned out, Lincoln's suspension of the writ of habeas corpus was only the beginning. He allowed military authorities in Maryland to arrest several pro-Confederate legislators when the Maryland legislature tried to reconvene in September, after rumors flared of a renewed attempt to pull the state out of the Union, coordinated with a possible Confederate invasion of the state. Available evidence suggests that this was done at the behest of local authorities rather than Lincoln himself.[38] Still, the president had set the tone for a muscular enforcement of wartime internal security. His July message to Congress made clear his belief that winning the war and safeguarding the

Union took top priority, sometimes at the expense of kicking over the traces. It was certainly understandable if his subordinates read his "all the laws but one" doctrine as an indication they should err on the side of caution when dealing with secessionists in the Border States, and "copperheads" in general.

And there were excesses. Some people were arrested with little good reason, and at times military authorities crossed the line between safeguarding national security and suppressing legitimate dissent. But serious scholars who have studied Lincoln's wartime internal security policies—historians like Mark Neely, who investigated the available documentary record in exhaustive detail—conclude that, on the whole, the arrests made under the Lincoln administration's policies were justifiable. Very few truly innocent people were persecuted, Lincoln and his subordinates strove to verify their suspicions with valid evidence, and they released their prisoners from custody soon after a perceived threat had passed.[39] John Merryman himself was freed in July 1861.[40]

The dire predictions of Roger Taney did not come true. The Constitution in the end proved far more adaptable than the chief justice and like-minded Americans realized. For all his posturing as the last best hope of constitutional liberty in America, Taney—unlike Lincoln—seems to have had little faith that the Constitution could bend without breaking. The war would prove him wrong.

CHAPTER SIX

CONGRESS AND WINNING THE WAR

There were Republicans who by the end of the war's first year believed the party had made a mistake by nominating such an untried, inexperienced man for the highest political office in the land. The glow of having captured the White House with Lincoln—at the helm of a party that was only six years old, no less—quickly faded. "It is a common thing to hear Republicans abuse the President and the Cabinet, as they would not allow a political opponent to do," noted one observer; "this comes, say the party, of choosing a fourth-rate man for President."[1]

Much of this criticism came from the more extreme wing of the Republican Party known as the Radicals. They were a powerful presence in Congress, led by Charles Sumner, Zachariah Chandler of Michigan, Thaddeus Stevens of Pennsylvania, Benjamin Wade of Ohio, and George Julian of Indiana. The Radicals tended to be severe, abrasive sorts, who developed reputations for brooking no compromise and giving the Confederates no quarter. "The South has got to be punished and traitors hung," Wade argued. In a similar vein, Sumner warned early in the war against any attempts at compromise or negotiation with Southerners. "Alas! It is ourselves that have encouraged the conspiracy [of secessionists] and made it strong. Secession has become possible only through long-continued concession. In proposing concession we have encouraged secession, and while professing to uphold the Union, we have betrayed it."[2]

Like the Radicals, Lincoln wanted a robust prosecution of the war, reworking his constitutional thought to encompass the Union as an aim of higher law, and formulating an expansive understanding of the Constitution that would allow him to do what was necessary to preserve the Union and fight the war. But his essentially modern conception of the importance of public opinion meant that he was unwilling to press too far ahead of what he thought mainstream Americans would bear. This very feature made him seem unbearably weak and timid to many Radicals.

Where Lincoln's differences with Taney involved him in a clash with the judiciary, Lincoln's differences with the Radical Republicans pushed him into differences of opinion and policy with Congress. The clash would not usually be so stark and direct as that between Lincoln and Taney; indeed, as the war progressed, Lincoln steadily gravitated towards the Radicals' point of view on a variety of matters. But this was not at first so clear—to the Radicals, the nation, or even Lincoln himself. As much trouble as Taney and other extreme strict constructionists might have caused, the Radicals in Congress kept him up nights, as well.

There was of course a great deal of common ground between Lincoln, the Radical Republicans, and more moderate Republicans; they were members of the same political party, after all. Much of that common ground concerned policies having little to do with slavery or race. In fact, many of these policies were not even directly related to the war. Quietly put into place while the battles raged, they were rooted in the Hamiltonian constitutionalism that animated both Lincoln and most members of his party.

Lincoln and his fellow Republicans had always seen western expansion as a vehicle for promoting American entrepreneurship and individual ambition and enterprise—the very antithesis of a slave-based economy, and a major reason why Lincoln and the Republicans so fiercely opposed slavery's expansion into the western territories. Republicans also thought it was the federal government's duty to actively promote the creation of a West filled with prosperous, independent farmers, beholden to no one and engaged in a robust market economy. This also was anathema to slaveholding Southerners, whose state sovereignty, strict constructionist constitutionalism denied the federal government any such role.

But now those slaveholding Southerners were mostly gone, fighting for the Confederacy. Republican congressmen—with the full support of their president—were free to act on their ambitions for federal involvement in the West. In May 1862, Congress passed the Homestead Act, which provided the legal mechanisms by which farmers could acquire farmland in the West at almost no cost to themselves—in effect, a giant land giveaway, sponsored by the federal government. Republicans justified the measure socially as a way of filling the West with solid, hardworking, independent farmers; they justified it politically as a way to cement the loyalty of those farmers to their party; and they justified it constitutionally by appealing to both the Constitution's Article IV, Section 3 power given to the federal government to regulate and dispose of public lands, and (in a more Hamiltonian, broad constructionist bent) the Constitution's empowerment of the federal government to provide for the "general welfare" of the American people.[3]

Congressional Republicans did not stop there. Over the course of the war, they created a variety of laws using robust federal power to stimulate economic development: a mainstay of Hamilton's constitutional thought, and unthinkable for strict constructionists in the Jeffersonian, Southern mold. Two months after passage of the Homestead Act, Congress created the Morrill Land-Grant Colleges Act, which awarded federal land to states that created colleges devoted primarily to "agriculture and the mechanic arts." Congress also created laws designed to modernize and improve the nation's archaic, decentralized, and (in a time of war) dangerously backward financial system: the National Banking Acts of 1863 and 1864, which established the national banking system that Lincoln and other old-line Whigs had been arguing for since the days of Andrew Jackson; and the Legal Tender Act of 1862, allowing the government to use paper money to pay its bills. Congress also saw fit to pass legislation designed to aid in the construction of a transcontinental railroad.

With all these laws, the United States finally created the uniform currency, financial system, and infrastructure appropriate for a burgeoning modern economy.[4]

Lincoln was a ready supporter of all these measures, albeit in a limited way. His direct involvement was circumscribed by the standards of his age. Presidents were not supposed to be very actively involved in the formation of domestic policy, which people tended to see as the prerogative of Congress. But Lincoln was quietly supportive. While he did not publicly address the constitutional issues involved—his predecessor, Democrat James Buchanan, had vetoed an early version of the Homestead Act on explicitly constitutional, strict constructionist grounds—Lincoln's willingness to quickly and without comment sign every one of these measures into law suggests that he agreed with Congress's policies and the robust constitutionalism that lay at their roots.

In many ways, then, Lincoln and his fellow congressional Republicans saw eye to eye. They shared common goals concerning partnership between the federal government and free enterprise, and they likewise bolstered these policies with a shared belief that the Constitution should be broadly interpreted in their favor.

But there were areas of disagreement and friction, as well. They were rooted not so much in terms of policy differences or the philosophical arguments between strict or broad construction of constitutional language, but rather in separation of powers issues, and the age-old tug-of-war between the presidency and Congress. The Constitution contains numerous potential flash points between the executive and legislative branches, areas of governance where the boundaries between the two are fuzzy and indistinct. War-making provided just such a flash point; and by the end of 1861, a charismatic young general highlighted that fact.

George Brinton McClellan was only thirty-four years old when he was appointed commander in chief of the Union army in November 1861. On paper, McClellan seemed the perfect man for the job, having commanded the Union army that cleared the Confederates out of western Virginia and paved the way for the region's eventual secession from Virginia and separate statehood. "We feel very proud of our wise and brave young Major-general," enthused the *New York Times*; "there is a future before him."[5]

But McClellan's rapid and unimpeded successes masked some underlying flaws. He was a curious mixture of arrogance and prudence, both of which he carried to excess. On the battlefield, this meant he could be both difficult to work with and unreasonably cautious.

Caution imbued his politics, as well. Little Mac was a conservative Democrat, who had many Southern friends before the war. He was deeply involved in the political landscape of wartime Washington, DC. He maintained regular contact with Democratic congressmen and the editors of prominent Democratic newspapers. While McClellan publicly denied any overt political ambitions, he also did little to discourage talk of his securing the party's presidential nomination in 1864.[6]

Did Lincoln take any of this seriously, to the point that he viewed McClellan as an out-and-out political rival in 1862? He never said as much. But McClellan did become a nexus of conflict between Lincoln and Congress, throwing into sharp relief the undeveloped constitutional questions concerning the relationship between the president and Congress during a war.

As the winter of 1861 turned into the spring of 1862, Congress grew impatient to see some sign of action from the army's chief commander. It seemed to many that he had no intention of actually using it—that in fact the entire Union war effort had more or less ground to a halt on McClellan's watch. And when he did try to act, McClellan seemed inordinately accident-prone. A Union force that landed at a place called Ball's Bluff near Leesburg, Virginia, in October, 1861, was surprised and badly mauled by a much larger Confederate force. The entire operation was poorly planned and executed, leaving Union soldiers with their backs to the river and no avenue of retreat. Nearly one thousand men were killed and captured, many by drowning as they desperately tried to reach boats dispatched to rescue them under heavy enemy fire. Some of the bodies floated down the Potomac and washed ashore at Washington, DC, bringing the grisly tragedy practically to the very doorstep of an increasingly frustrated federal government.

Ball's Bluff was also a private tragedy for Lincoln; one of his good friends from Illinois, Edward Baker, lost his life in the melee.[7] For his fellow Republicans in Congress, the debacle was the last straw. They were ready to press their claims for a larger degree of congressional leadership in the war effort.[8]

Congress had already taken a very active role in gearing the country for war. The Constitution tasked it generally with raising the army and navy, and during the war's first year, Congress put into place the vast and complex machinery for doing so: appropriations bills for purchasing muskets and other army equipment, constructing naval vessels, floating batteries and coastal fortifications, authorization of salary and pay levels for military personnel, setting uniform rules of conduct for soldiers, paymasters and military police . . . all the myriad operations required by a modern military establishment to prosecute a sprawling war effort. Relations between the president and Congress were generally amiable throughout, because none of these measures involved a serious clash between the two branches. Congress was doing what it was constitutionally supposed to do: create a military force for Lincoln, the commander in chief, to employ as he and his generals saw fit.[9]

But doubts about Lincoln's competence and McClellan's various shenanigans now caused many in Congress to wonder if they should become more actively involved in day-to-day military operations. Even those who were kindly disposed towards the president often thought of him as a lightweight, someone who could be easily led astray by more conservative voices in his cabinet, and perhaps by McClellan himself. "The President—and I do not mean to flatter—is as honest a man as there is in the world," declared Thaddeus Stevens, "but I believe him to be too easy and amiable."[10]

After Ball's Bluff, the Radicals in Congress felt the time had come for direct action. In December 1861, they created the Joint Committee on the Conduct of the War—"joint" because it included three senators and four representatives. Formed largely at the behest of Radical leaders (though disaffection with the war effort was so deep that most Democrats also voted for the measure), the joint committee was originally proposed as an investigative body for ascertaining precisely what had gone wrong in the two most embarrassing Union battlefield defeats—Bull Run and Ball's Bluff. But the committee's purview was quickly expanded to include investigative authority into any military matter it deemed worthy of inquiry.

There had been other such committees in the past, but those committees had been temporary and focused upon specific campaigns.[11] The new joint committee possessed an open-ended mandate, with no boundaries concerning what was and what was not its proper sphere. Some worried about the constitutionality of this, thinking that perhaps the committee would lead Congress to meddle in matters left by the Constitution in the hands of the "military authorities"— meaning the president as commander in chief and his generals. But these concerns were overridden by others who saw the committee's investigative work as directly germane to Congress's authority; and they emphasized the issue of precisely which branch of the federal government most directly represented the interests of the people during a people's contest. "We are placing a great burden upon the people of this country," noted William Pitt Fessenden of Maine, "and while we are their agents (because it is in Congress to declare war, and in providing the means to carry on the war), it behooves us most carefully to look at the course of proceedings related to the conduct of the war."[12]

Fessenden's point was technically doubtful, since Congress never declared war against the Confederacy (how could it do so when the Confederacy did not legally exist as a nation?). But on a broader scale, his remarks were telling, for they highlighted an important question: Which branch of government was primarily responsible for the day-to-day decisions necessary to fight a large-scale war?

Lincoln's answer was, emphatically, himself. From the war's outset, he was very much a hands-on commander in chief, involving himself deeply in day-to-day military operations. This was not always a good thing, as he had a tendency to sometimes fritter his time away with minutiae that was better delegated elsewhere—reflecting his lack of real administrative experience before entering the White House. It also reflected the lack of good leadership at the top of the War Department's chain of command. Lincoln's first secretary of war, Simon Cameron, was a Pennsylvania politician with little experience or expertise in military matters, and soon his department was rife with incompetence and outright corruption.[13]

In those early days, Lincoln may well have felt the need to step in and take charge simply because Cameron was so obviously and so badly out of his depth. When he eventually replaced Cameron with the hard-driving, no-nonsense Edwin M. Stanton in early 1862, Lincoln was able to step back at least a bit and allow Stanton to take over. But the president was still given to monitoring the details of military operations, everything from soldiers' punishments for desertion to testing new military weapons on the White House lawn.[14]

He took his constitutional prerogatives as commander in chief quite seriously and was not much given to deferring those powers elsewhere, either within his own administration or in the legislative branch. As we have seen, Congress was also heavily involved from the outset with managing the war's endless tasks, as befitted its constitutional prerogatives for raising an army and a navy, and making the rules by which they operated. For the most part, the twin constitutional heads of the Union's war-making apparatus, Lincoln and Congress, functioned well.

But the joint committee was another matter. Congress would now reassert itself by acting the part of the people's inquisitor into a war effort that had been left exclusively in the hands of the chief executive—and which seemed to have gone badly awry. It seemed to represent an open challenge to Lincoln's role as commander in chief by asserting a mandate for Congress to intrude itself upon the daily command and control decisions heretofore reserved entirely for the president.

The Joint Committee on the Conduct of the War opened for business on December 9, 1861, looking first into the circumstances surrounding the Bull Run defeat, and then investigating what went wrong at Ball's Bluff. The committee gathered a variety of eyewitness testimonies, including that of several high-ranking army officers. McClellan himself was called for an informal interview with committee members in January—a "general consultation" that did not carry the weight of a formal subpoena, but was nevertheless part of the committee's open-ended investigation process.[15]

Inevitably the committee's inquiries led to areas that looked much more like the proper purview of a commander in chief, rather than Congress: battlefield tactics, supply and support issues, questions concerning proper training and army discipline, and the authority of a given commander to order a withdrawal or an attack. The committee did not acquit itself well when it delved into these issues, which was hardly surprising, since few of its members possessed any real military expertise. They were prone to second-guessing decisions made under trying battlefield conditions; casting unnecessary aspersions upon officers with West Point training (the Radicals saw the military academy as a bastion of pro-Southern conservatism); and critiquing complex operations with an almost willful lack of appreciation for the problems inherent in waging modern war.[16]

Along with its members' lack of military knowledge, the committee left itself open to charges that it was engaged in a partisan witch hunt. The committee's Radical Republican members, led by chairman Ben Wade, equated cowardice, incompetence, and possibly even treason with the Democratic politics of some generals, while at the same time praising the vigor and energy of those officers whose loyalties leaned towards the Republicans. A general with the proper Republican zeal for the war, they reasoned, should be able to overcome any battlefield obstacle; breathtaking presumption this was, coming in particular from men who had never seen a Civil War battlefield.

Anyone connected with George McClellan received particularly rough handling by the committee, as did the general himself. During his quasi-formal January interview, Zachariah Chandler asked McClellan why he did not immediately attack the Rebels; McClellan replied he was awaiting the construction of several bridges across the Potomac River, to give his army an avenue of retreat if necessary—a perfectly plausible response, given that the lack of such an option contributed to the Ball's Bluff mess. But Chandler was unimpressed. "If I understand you correctly, before you strike at the rebels you want to be sure of plenty of room so that you can run in case they strike back!" he retorted. "Or in case you get scared," sneered Wade. Offended, Little Mac tried to defend himself, then stalked angrily from the room. "Chandler, what do you think of the science of generalship?" Wade then asked. "I don't know much about war," Chandler replied, "but it seems to me that this is infernal, unmitigated cowardice."[17]

For his part, McClellan despised the committee—hardly surprising, since Little Mac heartily disapproved of the Radical Republicans and all their works. He was also disinclined to look with favor upon any civilian meddling in military affairs, an attitude the general shared with nearly all professional soldiers, then and since. When McClellan fell ill with fever in December 1861, rumor had it in Washington, DC, that he was faking sickness to avoid having to appear before the committee, which had summoned him. "I am so much better this morning that I am going before the Joint Committee," he wrote Lincoln on January 15, adding with a bit of gallows humor, "if I escape alive I will report when I get through."[18]

The committee soon found itself in a state of war against McClellan and his conservative Democratic friends in the Union army high command. If the Founding Fathers ever seriously contemplated a larger role for Congress in the day-to-day operations of war, a peek into the future at the heavily politicized and often counterproductive partisanship of the joint committee would have surely given them pause. However well-intentioned and understandable Congress's actions might have been in forming the committee—and however much George McClellan in some respects deserved the scrutiny—its proceedings were disturbingly ill-informed and divisive. "Members of the Joint Committee on the Conduct of the War worked long and hard on their assignments," wrote historian Bruce Tap in his exhaustive study of the Committee. "No one could accuse them of shirking their duty. They were patriotic; they wanted to win the war. . . . [But] the result of their interference spawned distrust and jealousies among the top Union military commanders, helped undermine bipartisan support for the war, increased popular misconceptions about the nature of warfare, and contributed to the politicization of military appointments."[19]

In fairness, as Tap points out, the committee did involve itself in useful labor for the war effort, of the sort that escaped the scrutiny of the press and much of the country. While their investigations of prominent Union generals made headlines, the committee also held hearings regarding more mundane—but vital—military matters. They ferreted out abuse and mismanagement in the army's and navy's vast and ever-expanding supply and logistics machinery. They also investigated reports of battlefield atrocities committed by Confederates against African American soldiers and used the committee as a powerful platform to highlight the dangers faced by black soldiers as they faced an implacable Southern enemy.[20]

These matters fell more directly within Congress's constitutional sphere, for the Constitution did empower Congress to oversee the various administrative details of the war. But nothing the committee tried to do could be divorced from what had become a tense political atmosphere. For example, the committee recommended to McClellan that he reorganize the army along the lines of the French corps system, a move that was also plausibly within Congress's constitutional boundaries and had some military merit. But it would also (not coincidentally) have required the shuffling and removal of several McClellan cronies from the army's command structure. Not surprisingly McClellan balked at the idea; and (also not surprisingly) the committee's Radical members expressed their belief that Little Mac was ignoring a sound administrative change merely to protect his friends.[21]

What did Lincoln think of the joint committee?

For the most part, Lincoln observed a discreet silence. He rarely mentioned the committee in his public speeches and messages to Congress. He sometimes met with committee members on a quasi-formal basis at the White House, and when he received a request from the committee for such a meeting, he complied with no apparent unease or open hostility. He also cooperated with the smaller and lesser-known congressional committees created to address abuses and corruption in military contracting procedures and other financial aspects of the war.[22]

A lesser politician might have chosen to throw down the gauntlet to the committee; it was powerful, but as president and leader of the Republican Party, Lincoln wielded his share of weapons, as well. Had he wanted to do so, he could have used his patronage powers and general political influence to blunt the committee's authority. He could have stonewalled the committee's requests for meetings, or he might have tried to block the committee's access to military channels of information necessary for their investigations. He could have refused to meet with them at all.

Lincoln had some constitutional justification for doing so. The argument could have been made that the joint committee was impinging upon Lincoln's constitutional duties as commander in chief, particularly when it chose to investigate the more minute operations of the army and navy. Lincoln might have invoked executive privilege to keep Congress at arm's length. Given how closely the committee was identified with the Radicals, he would have garnered at least some political support among more moderate and conservative Americans had he chosen to do so.

Privately, the president may well have found the committee irksome, though direct evidence is lacking. When committee members met with the president to urge adoption of their new army reorganization plan, Lincoln merely responded blandly that he had never really given the matter much thought. He sometimes was quietly uncooperative when the committee or Congress pursued investigation of military affairs. When the Senate passed a resolution on December 17 (a week after the joint committee was formally created) requesting information from Secretary of War Simon Cameron concerning the conduct of General James Patterson at the Battle of Bull Run, Cameron refused to comply. Lincoln's exact role in this matter is unclear, but it is hard to imagine Cameron taking such action without at least the president's tacit approval.[23]

But Lincoln studiously avoided an open rift. He continued to meet with committee members informally, as circumstances warranted. Later in the war, the president authorized cabinet and staff members to cooperate with the committee's deliberations. When the committee opened an investigation into the Union defeat at the Battle of Olustee, Florida, in March 1864—a defeat that was particularly disturbing to some Radicals, since it involved African Americans serving in the famous Fifty-Fourth Massachusetts Volunteer Infantry—Secretary of War Edwin Stanton dutifully supplied the committee with copies of paperwork associated with that battle. Lincoln allowed the committee's investigation to proceed without comment or interference.[24]

This was vintage Lincoln: a behind-the-scenes, nonconfrontational, and pragmatic approach that avoided an outright showdown with Congress. Lincoln's relationship with Congress and the joint committee proved that his constitutional elasticity cut both ways. If it could expand regarding such issues as the habeas corpus controversy, then it could also contract when circumstances required. In this ability to both expand and contract, to act with both boldness and circumspection, Lincoln found a true middle ground during the war.

LINCOLN AND THE RADICALS

Privately, Lincoln abhorred slavery; his record during the sectional crises of the 1850s made this abundantly clear. But political reality did not allow him to walk the walk of the Radicals, nearly all of whom wanted both an end to the war and some form of racial equality. They could afford more extreme positions on race and slavery because they represented relatively narrow constituencies in their districts who more or less expected them to stake out such positions. But Lincoln was president of the entire country. He was compelled by the structure of his office to take into account the wishes and feelings of more moderate and conservative Northerners.

The elasticity in Lincoln's constitutional thought, generated by the war's give-and-take, would be tested to its limit by the vexing, complex, and hyperemotional issue of emancipation. Habeas corpus and the war's internal security needs compelled Lincoln to expand his reading of presidential authority. Congress's desire to become more actively involved the war effort, and the attendant political issues, caused Lincoln to tread even more carefully. Emancipation required Lincoln to act both with energy and circumspection, boldness and caution.

Lincoln tried during the first year of the war to avoid slavery as an issue altogether. But slavery was not such an easy thing to avoid; it surfaced constantly, especially on the battle front. As Union armies advanced into the South, their very presence rattled and shook loose slavery's foundations. Runaway slaves increasingly found their way

into Union army camps, despite the fact that no Northern authority had promised them freedom. "I wanted to see these wonderful
'Yankees' so much, as I heard my parents say the Yankee was going
to set all the slaves free," recalled Susie King, a young slave girl
who escaped to the Union army at Fort Pulaski, Georgia, in April
1862—five months before the federal government announced that
emancipation was official Union policy.[1]

No one quite knew what to do with the Susie Kings of the South.
More politically conservative commanders returned fugitive slaves to
their masters, George McClellan being the most prominent example
(and yet another reason he drew the Radicals' ire). But this became an
increasingly unsettling solution, even to those Americans who cared
little about African Americans. Everyone knew Southerners employed
slaves to dig fortifications, drive wagons, repair roads, and perform
the myriad other labors required by a modern army. By returning
runaway slaves, many wondered, were they not in effect strengthen-
ing the enemy? And did not the Confederates deserve to lose their
"property"? Handing a slave back to the enemy was not far removed
from giving the enemies back their guns; and it was this very sort of
analogy that sparked one early solution to the problem—a solution
by, of all people, a cross-eyed, dyspeptic politician-turned-general
named Benjamin Butler.

Butler was a difficult, abrasive, and (some said) corrupt Democrat
from Massachusetts. He was utterly inept on the battlefield, but he
was a first-rate attorney. When runaways began streaming into his
lines in the area around Norfolk, Virginia, where he commanded
Union forces, he turned his lawyer's-eye view to the problem. A
Confederate officer had appeared under flag of truce in May 1861
demanding the return of three runaways; Butler retorted that he
would "hold these Negroes as contraband of war, since they are engaged in the construction of your [artillery] battery and are claimed
as your property." To Butler's way of thinking, he could seize and
keep runaway slaves with the same legal and practical reasoning he
could use to seize and keep a captured enemy cannon or musket.
It was an ingenious solution to the runaway problem, and many
Northerners chuckled at the irony of classifying slaves as property in

order to treat them with some measure of humanity. "Contraband" quickly became the slang term of choice to describe runaway slaves.[2]

But calling a fugitive slave a "contraband" did not confer freedom. It simply meant that the runaway was no longer owned by a Rebel master. If the master did not therefore own the runaway slave, and if the runaway was not legally free, then what was his or her status?

Congress tried to address the situation when it passed the Property Confiscation Act in August 1861. The act was designed to clarify the legal status of all property captured by Union authorities in the course of the war, not just slaves. But the last paragraph stated that any slave put to work "upon any fort, navy yard, dock, armory, ship, entrenchment, or in any military or naval service whatsoever, against the Government and lawful authority of the United States, then, and in every such case, the person to whom such labor or service is claimed to be due shall forfeit his claim to such labor, any law of the State or of the United States to the contrary notwithstanding."[3] Lincoln worried about the political fallout that could arise from the bill, particularly in the Border States, but in the end he signed it into law.

The Confiscation Act really did not settle the basic problem: Were runaway slaves free? Again, no one really knew. The law terminated the property right that a disloyal slaveholder held in the runaway slave, but it did not then automatically confer freedom on the runaway. Contrabands were now the property of the US government—a most awkward situation.

Congress tried to further clarify the slaves' status a year later with the Second Confiscation Act. The first Confiscation Act had declared only that Rebel slaveholders could not retrieve their runaways; the Second Act clearly stated that those slaves would now be freed, making explicit what the first act had implied. This applied only to Rebel slaveholders, and it gave even those individuals sixty days to lay down their arms and rejoin the Union. Still, the Second Confiscation Act was a significant step in the general direction of freeing the slaves: a dress rehearsal for emancipation, so to speak. And it was widely perceived as a predominantly Radical measure, even though it was written only after lengthy and contentious negotiations in the Congress between Republican Radicals and moderates.

But Lincoln was worried. Part of the problem lay in the fact that the Second Confiscation Act clearly and unambiguously freed fugitive slaves and extinguished their owners' claims to their human "property." He was not troubled by this, but he did know that taking away slave "property," under any circumstances, might cause constitutional problems. The Founding Fathers elevated individual property rights to a specially protected status in the Constitution's Bill of Rights, specifically the Fifth Amendment, which held that no person could be deprived of "life, liberty, or property" by the federal government without "due process of law." "Due process" was subject to different interpretations, but the language meant in effect that the federal courts—and most especially the Taney-led Supreme Court—could be expected to hold any government action depriving Southerners of their property to a very high standard. Justice Taney laid the groundwork for this in *Dred Scott v. Sanford*, when he ruled that the Fifth Amendment made property protection an almost sacred constitutional value. Lincoln had good reason to worry that any measure enacted by Congress (or, for that matter, by Lincoln himself) that took slaves away from their masters stood a good chance of being struck down by the Supreme Court as a violation of the masters' due process rights.

Lincoln's chief worry about the act concerned the Constitution's treason language, contained in Article III, Section 3, which held that "no Attainder of Treason shall work Corruption of Blood, or Forfeiture except during the Life of the Person attainted."[4] The Second Confiscation Act explicitly used the word "treason" to describe a person fighting for the Confederacy, and then declared that "all his slaves, if any, shall be declared and made free." Presumably, those slaves would remain free thereafter. Lincoln worried that this amounted to forfeiture after "the life of the person attainted." "With great respect, I am constrained to say I think this feature of the act is unconstitutional," Lincoln wrote in a message to Congress in which he stated his concerns.[5]

In voicing these objections, Lincoln once again drew upon the constitutional elasticity that characterized his relations with Congress. A more ham-fisted president might have simply vetoed the Confiscation Act outright, thereby provoking Congress—especially the Radicals—into an equally harsh response. Instead, Lincoln drafted a list of his objections, which was not quite a veto, and which was couched in the most respectful language possible. He then gave Congress to understand that, if his concerns were properly addressed, he would sign the bill. After a series of hastily convened negotiations between congressional leaders and the president, Congress amended the law to indicate that no property would be seized beyond the lifetime of any given Confederate property owner. Lincoln then signed the Second Confiscation Act into law.

Lincoln acted with restraint and forbearance, avoiding an ugly confrontation with Congress by sidling right up to the edge of a veto while avoiding an open break. On the other hand, Lincoln saw to it that his objections were recorded and his list of objections made public, even after Congress had made them moot by amending their bill. In doing so, he annoyed many Radicals, even as he may have at least partially reassured moderates and conservatives that he would not unthinkingly bend to the Radicals' will.[6]

The Radicals did have allies in the field. In August 1861, General John C. Fremont, an antislavery man and the Union commander of the Department of Missouri, cracked down on the state's increasingly recalcitrant Rebel sympathizers by declaring martial law and confiscating Rebel-owned property, including slaves. Fremont did not temporize about their status, either; the Rebels' "slaves, if any they have, shall be declared freemen."[7]

His proclamation created a national sensation. Fremont "has immortalized himself as the only man in power who thoroughly understood the necessities of the occasion and had the courage to meet them," enthused a supporter in New York; he was "the people's first leader against the great slaveholder's conspiracy, [and] has been the first man to strike the first great blow against its bold outbreak." But the proclamation did not play nearly so well elsewhere, especially in the Border States. "It is dangerous and odious," wrote the editor of the *Louisville (Kentucky) Journal*, "and, we trust, will be promptly repudiated by the Government."[8]

The *Journal* knew what it was about. Fremont had not consulted Lincoln. The president saw the proclamation as at best premature, and at worse a provocation to the Border State slaveholders and other conservatives whose cooperation was necessary to win the war. Always careful to avoid open confrontation, Lincoln gave Fremont an opportunity to modify his own proclamation, and thus save both men from the appearance of an open rift. "I think there is great danger that . . . liberating slaves of traiterous [*sic*] owners, will alarm our Southern Union friends, and turn them against us—perhaps ruin our rather fair prospect for Kentucky," Lincoln wrote Fremont three days after the proclamation was issued. He asked the general to rewrite the proclamation rescinding its emancipationist language and closed with reassurance that "this letter is written in a spirit of caution and not of censure."[9]

Fremont was not the sort who responded well to conciliation. He refused to alter the proclamation, forcing an annoyed Lincoln to directly order Fremont to rescind the Proclamation.[10] He struck down Fremont's proclamation for the same reason he objected to the Second Confiscation Act: He believed Fremont had violated the Constitution's ban on punishing treason beyond the life of the traitor. If the army took a person's farm or pasture for its own use, then that was a temporary matter of military occupation—the owner would get his or her property back eventually—and was acceptable under military law. The same held true for slaves, but only to a point. "If the General needs them, he can seize them, and use them," Lincoln argued, "but when the need is past, it is not for him to fix their permanent future condition. That must be settled according to laws made by law-makers, and not by military proclamations."

Lincoln's reference to "law-makers" pointed to another serious constitutional issue, one that actually had little to do with slavery: civilian control of the military. Fremont's actions usurped the author-ity of the president and Congress to make such sweeping decisions. "The proclamation in the point in question, is simply 'dictatorship,'" he wrote. "It assumes that the general may do *anything* he pleases— confiscate the lands and free the slaves of *loyal* people, as well as of disloyal ones. Can it be pretended that it is any longer the government of the US—any government of Constitution and laws?"[11]

Lincoln paid a stiff price in Radical circles for his revocation of the Fremont proclamation. While some defended the president as perhaps overcautious but a fellow traveler at heart, others denounced him as a coward. Benjamin Wade privately sneered that Lincoln's actions were only what one might expect of a man who was "born of poor white trash, and educated in a slave state." Other antislavery-minded Northerners were likewise incensed. "In the recent proclamation of Gen. Fremont . . . we saw a harbinger of better days and the surest means, to bring this war to a speedy close," bemoaned a meeting of German Americans in Chicago, and they were dismayed that it "was unfortunately mutilated by the order of the President."[12]

Nine months later, another Union general, David Hunter, tried the president on the same point. Commander of Union forces in South Carolina, Hunter was (like Fremont) an antislavery man who also worried about the increasing manpower problems faced by the Union army. He began recruiting soldiers from the ranks of fugitive slaves and in May 1862, declared martial law in his department. "Slavery and martial law in a free country are altogether incompatible," Hunter (rather oddly) argued, and he announced that the persons in Georgia, Florida, and South Carolina "heretofore held as slaves, are therefore declared forever free."[13]

Lincoln's response was much the same. Chagrined by Fremont's behavior, the president did not even give Hunter the option of modifying the order; he simply quashed it. "I further make known that whether it be competent for me, as Commander-in-Chief of the Army and Navy, to declare the Slaves of any state or states, free . . . are questions which, under my responsibility, I reserve to myself, and which I can not feel justified in leaving to the decision of commanders in the field," Lincoln wrote in a public announcement intended to mollify the "excitement, and misunderstanding" of Hunter's decree.[14]

Lincoln's objections to Fremont and Hunter did not concern the morality of slavery, for on that level there was very little difference between them. The issue was political—preserving the fragile loyalty of Northern conservatives and the slaveholding Border States—and especially constitutional. However well-intentioned Fremont and Hunter might have been, and however much Lincoln may have privately sympathized with their aims, he saw their actions as a threat to the time-honored American principle of civilian control over the military. "No commanding general shall do such a thing, upon *my* responsibility, without consulting me," he exclaimed to Chase.[15]

In the meantime, a sea change was quietly occurring in the Northern populace, and in the army's rank and file. Many soldiers had become convinced that emancipation was the only way to hurt the Confederacy enough to compel their surrender. "There is nothing [the Rebels] seem to feel so much, and care so much about, as to lose their slaves," remarked one private. "I honestly believe that many of them would rather have us *kidnap their children*, than to *let* their niggers go off with us."[16]

Still, Lincoln had good reason to proceed carefully. If there were many white Northerners now willing to end slavery, there were also many others who cared nothing for either slavery or African Americans generally; Lincoln could not well ignore them. Nor could he be sure which sentiment would prevail in the ongoing struggle to engage Northerners' hearts and minds, and keep them motivated to continue the conflict. Emancipation might energize enough people to win the war, or it might alienate enough people to lose the war. Lincoln could not be sure which.

On the surface, he seemed to be a bundle of contradictions, directionless and unsure what to do about the slavery question, and hopelessly enthralled by conservatives. "We think you are unduly influenced by the counsels, the representations, the menaces of certain fossil politicians hailing from the Border Slave states," complained *New York Tribune* editor Horace Greeley in his famous letter "The Prayer of Twenty Millions," urging Lincoln to free the slaves. "We think timid counsels in such a crisis [are] calculated to prove perilous, and probably disastrous."[17]

Lincoln was actually moving, steadily and very quietly, in the direction of emancipation—he had already composed a draft of the Emancipation Proclamation, in fact, even as Greeley wrote those words. But Lincoln did not see fit to let the *Tribune*'s editor or the American public in on this secret. He wrote a subtly crafted reply to Greeley that was a masterpiece of political gamesmanship. "If there be those who would not save the Union, unless they could at the same time *save* slavery, I do not agree with them," Lincoln wrote, and "if there be those who would not save the Union unless they could at the same time *destroy* slavery, I do not agree with them. My paramount object in this struggle *is* to save the Union, and is *not* either to save or to destroy slavery. If I could save the Union without freeing *any* slave I would do it, and if I could save it by freeing *all* the slaves I would do it; and if I could save it by freeing some and leaving others alone I would also do that."[18]

This letter was widely read and reprinted around the country, as Lincoln intended; and what it signified depended upon the eye of the beholder. It could plausibly be taken as reluctance to do anything at all about slavery, and it could just as plausibly indicate a willingness on Lincoln's part to pursue emancipation. Most of all, it was entirely consistent with Lincoln's decision, at the outbreak of the war, to make the Union his highest goal, the "apple of gold."

But those who read his response to the Greeley letter as an either/ or choice between the Union or emancipation, as if the former were an affirmation of slavery, misunderstood Lincoln's constitutional thought. For Lincoln, the natural end of the "Union," properly understood was, eventually, the demise of slavery and affirmation of liberty. He read the Founding Fathers' legacy in this manner, and he always thought the Union they created in Philadelphia in 1787 (which he habitually collapsed into the Union created by the Declaration of Independence in 1776) was by definition a national community that was fundamentally incompatible with human bondage, just as a cancerous tumor was incompatible with a human body.

When he posed a choice between Union or emancipation to Horace Greeley, he did not pose a choice between slavery and freedom; rather, he posed a choice between a Union that must eventually lead to slavery's demise, or some sort of immediate presidential executive order, issued by Lincoln in his capacity as commander in chief.

For decades, historians have wondered why Lincoln penned this sort of response to Horace Greeley when he already knew he was going to free the slaves. On a constitutional level, the seeming inconsistency between Lincoln's affirmation of the Union as his top priority and his simultaneous embrace of emancipation was no inconsistency at all. To him, *both* the Union and his Emancipation Proclamation inexorably led to slavery's demise, one quickly the other more slowly. They were simply different means to the same end.

That question of means was no small thing; indeed, to a harried and harassed president, beset on all sides by critics, enemies, and uncertainty, means mattered a great deal. Given a preference, Lincoln would have much preferred a peacetime Union bringing about the gradual eradication of slavery, as opposed to a wartime presidential edict that suddenly wrenched the institution loose.

Why? On a constitutional level, Lincoln worried about the short-term, temporary nature of any presidential emancipation, because any such order could have only one constitutional justification: war. And the war could not last forever.

Nothing in Article II's enumeration of presidential powers stated that a president could emancipate slaves. The most a peacetime president might hope to accomplish on his own would be offering suggestions to Congress that it act to ban slavery in those few areas over which it had direct authority: Washington, DC; the western territories; or perhaps the buying and selling of slaves between the states, which could arguably fall within the purview of the Constitution's commerce clause. But these would be suggestions only; as Lincoln himself noted in December 1860 (after he was elected, but before the war had begun), "I have no thought of recommending the abolition of slavery in the District of Columbia, nor the slave trade among the slave states, . . . and if I were to make such recommendation, it is quite clear Congress would not follow it."[19]

War, however, opened an entirely different constitutional dimension. "I felt that measures, otherwise unconstitutional, might become lawful, by becoming indispensable to the preservation of the constitution, through the preservation of the nation," Lincoln argued—the chief measure in question being emancipation.[20]

Americans generally agreed that in wartime, a president's war-making powers were considerable. This, along with Butler's contraband stratagem and the Confiscation Acts lit the path towards presidential emancipation: free the slaves by executive decree as a necessary war measure, in much the same way a military commander ordered troops to seize a musket or a cannon.

But "necessary" was a loaded constitutional term, fraught with controversy. Over the years, broad constructionists had often seized upon the "necessary and proper" clause as open-ended constitutional language that could be used to justify expansion of federal power. Conversely, strict constructionists saw any such use of the "necessary and proper" clause as inherently suspicious. "The plea of necessity is ever the tyrant's plea," or so an old saying went.

Whenever Lincoln invoked wartime "necessity," he invoked a concept that had roiled American constitutional thought since the nation's founding. The key constitutional question he therefore had to answer in relation to any emancipation decree was: Could emancipation be justified as a necessary war measure, and therefore an acceptable exercise of Lincoln's Article II, Section 2 powers as commander in chief?

Lincoln had reached a certain point by the summer of 1862: a point of critical mass, when all of the war's problems—battlefield stalemate, manpower losses, sagging civilian morale—propelled him towards making the bold move of presidential emancipation. "Things had gone from bad to worse, until I felt we had reached the end of our rope," Lincoln later recalled; "we had about played our last card, and must change our tactics, or lose the game [so] I now determined upon the adoption of the emancipation policy."[21]

Lincoln was no doubt telling the truth here, and he was also being entirely honest when he later told a critic of his emancipation policies, "I claim not to have controlled events, but confess plainly that events have controlled me. . . . I was, in my best judgment, driven to the alternative of either surrendering the Union, and with it, the Constitution, or of laying strong hand upon the colored element. I chose the latter."[22] He surely felt as if he had been more or less cornered by the war's many pressures into pursuing the risky and controversial policy of presidential emancipation.

But we would be doing Lincoln a disservice if we did not also note that he acted out of genuine moral conviction. His sense of right and wrong was an indispensable feature of his constitutional thought; it always had been. And now, one year into the war, he abolished slavery as both a military necessity and the right thing to do.

He proceeded carefully. One month after his reply to Horace Greeley, Lincoln issued a preliminary emancipation proclamation that gave the Rebels until the end of 1862 to return peaceably to the Union. If they chose to do so, they could keep their slaves—although Lincoln also indicated he would recommend Congress and the states adopt a plan of gradual, compensated emancipation. But on January 1, 1863, Lincoln continued, he would issue a second proclamation, freeing all the slaves in the rebellious states. He offered no overt constitutional justification for this action, beyond invoking in the first sentence of the proclamation his status as commander in chief of the nation's armed forces. He also took pains to cite chapter and verse of the Confiscation Acts by way of illustrating the consistency between his emancipation decree and Congress's actions.[23]

Clearly Lincoln preferred to spread the responsibility for emancipation around as much as possible, making it a policy undertaken by government, and not just by the executive branch. In the waning months of 1862, he tried in vain to persuade Border State congressmen to enact emancipation plans of their own. And as the January 1 deadline for his proclamation approached, he tried one last time to avoid the unknown and hazardous territory of presidential emancipation by proposing in his annual message to Congress a lengthy and elaborate emancipation scheme, one that might supersede and largely nullify his own upcoming Emancipation Proclamation.

Lincoln's proposal to Congress had a lot of moving parts, including two constitutional amendments—a rarity of itself; before Lincoln, no sitting president except James Madison had ever proposed an amendment to the Constitution—which would have required each state to abolish slavery by the year 1900; it meted out US Treasury bonds to compensate loyal slaveholders for their monetary loss and it appropriated money to encourage voluntary colonization of free African Americans to some undisclosed future location "at any place or places without the United States."[24]

Colonization and compensated emancipation were a soothing syrup Lincoln hoped might allow white Northerners to swallow what was to many the bitter pill of black freedom. Colonization was the favorite scheme of Lincoln's hero, Henry Clay, and Lincoln himself had spoken favorably of the idea since the early 1850s. Compensation was his way of heading off a possible legal crisis; give slaveholders a fair price for their lost "property," and they would be less likely (or able) to challenge emancipation in court as an unjust act of confiscation violating the Fifth Amendment's due process clause.

That soothing syrup would go down even more easily if administered by Congress as well as the White House. Lincoln wanted from these proposals a sense of shared responsibility between the two branches, the better to head off further charges of presidential tyranny and dictatorship. Congress was, after all, the people's branch of government; any emancipation plan emanating from that quarter would carry a more impressive imprimatur of democratic approval, all the more so because, unlike an executive order, congressional emancipation would not be solely the by-product of war. "Is it doubted that we here—Congress and Executive—can secure its adoption?" Lincoln asked. "Will not the good people respond to a united, and earnest appeal from us? Can we, can they, by any other means, so certainly, or so speedily, assure these vital objects? We can succeed only by concert." He closed his appeal with a ringing, eloquent Lincolnian appeal: "In *giving* freedom to the *slave*, we *assure* freedom to the *free*—honorable alike in what we give, and what we preserve. We shall nobly save, or meanly lose, the last best, hope of earth. Other means may succeed; this could not fail. The way is plain, peaceful, generous, just—a way which, if followed, the world will forever applaud, and God must forever bless."[25]

Despite his eloquence, the president's efforts met with dismal failure. Congress failed to act on Lincoln's proposals, and the Border State politicians with whom Lincoln conferred in the waning days of 1862 did not seriously pursue any sort of voluntary emancipation scheme.

In retrospect, Lincoln's efforts here seemed confusing to many people, both then and since. Was he committed to using his presidential powers as commander in chief to ensure a slave-free, multiracial American future, or not? In his intense pursuit of various colonization schemes, it seemed not. His attempts in his December congressional address to compensate slaveholders, and to postpone the final end of slavery until 1900, likewise suggested that he was far more interested in protecting white interests than serving the cause of racial equality. In all of his talk about the costs and compensation of emancipation, Lincoln never spoke of compensating African Americans for their many years of toil.

In fact, throughout that entire agonizing summer and fall of 1862, as Lincoln seemed buffeted back and forth by the various forces swirling around the emancipation issue, Lincoln said nothing much at all about what the Constitution did or did not do for black people, enslaved or free. He did not publicly invoke the Declaration of Independence as a touchstone of equality—as he had so often before the war—and in one widely publicized meeting with a deputation of African American leaders, he coldly stated that everyone would benefit if blacks simply left the country. "It is better for us both, therefore, to be separated," he declared. Lincoln even seemed to suggest that African Americans were responsible for the war. "But for your race among us there could not be war, although many men engaged on either side do not care for you one way or the other," he said. "Nevertheless, I repeat, without the institution of Slavery and the colored race as a basis, the war could not have an existence."[26]

Despite the attempts of subsequent generations to make Lincoln into a cardboard figure—the Great Emancipator, with no flaws, doubts, shortcomings, or mistakes—the simple fact was that Lincoln was groping—groping for victory in an increasingly brutal war, groping towards some new vision of a slave-free America that might or might not include some version of racial equality, groping perhaps also for a new sense of himself as a white man who had lived an entire life to that point privileged and protected by his white skin. It is hardly surprising that he said and did contradictory things, that he could pursue a policy placing the presidency at the leading edge of emancipation policy while simultaneously asking Congress and the states to in effect let him off the hook.

By the end of 1862, Lincoln had found within himself the wherewithal to fight the war. He had also found within himself the willingness to expand government power when necessary, sometimes to unprecedented levels. Now, at the most critical moment of all, he needed to find within himself the strength to do what was necessary

—to free the slaves with no help from Congress, certainly no help from the Supreme Court, no help from the states governments, and in the face of a divided, heavily bigoted white Northern public. "Object whatsoever is possible, still the question recurs, 'can we do better?,'" he declared to Congress in his December message. "The dogmas of the quiet past are inadequate to the stormy present. The occasion is piled high with difficulty, and we must rise with the occasion."[27]

And on January 1, 1863, Lincoln did so, signing the final Emancipation Proclamation into law. As with the preliminary document, Lincoln placed his constitutional war powers front and center as the wellspring of his authority to free the slaves "as a fit and necessary war measure for suppressing said rebellion." When at the end of the proclamation he invoked the blessing of God, he did so stating that he "sincerely believed [Emancipation] to be an act of justice, warranted by the Constitution [and] upon military necessity." While some viewed invocation of military necessity as signifying Lincoln's straitjacketed and narrow approach to emancipation—in effect saying, "the war made me do it"—those more familiar with America's constitutional tradition surely knew otherwise, knew that Lincoln's use of the word "necessity," placed him foursquare in the company of broad constructionists in the Alexander Hamilton mold who had always seen necessity as an enabler of robust American constitutionalism.[28] Still, Lincoln's emancipation moment was not an unbridled act of constitutional power. The Constitution provided the source of Lincoln's emancipation powers but it also defined its limitations. Lincoln excluded the Border States, as well as those areas then under direct Union control, in part because of his ever-present concern about the Fifth Amendment's due process clause, and what might happen if a hostile Supreme Court ever was given the opportunity to pass judgment on the proclamation.

Whatever its strengths and weaknesses, Lincoln knew the Emancipation Proclamation was the defining act of his presidency; and once he had committed himself and the country to emancipation, Lincoln would not retreat. He could have done so. The proclamation was only an executive order, which Lincoln could have revoked at any time. Some advised him to do that very thing, particularly when it appeared as if emancipation might do the Republicans serious harm at the polls. But Lincoln steadfastly refused. "Broken eggs can not be mended," he said. "I have issued the emancipation proclamation, and I can not retract it." Once African American soldiers shed blood in battle, he was even more forceful. "There have been men who have proposed to me to return to slavery the black warriors of Port Hudson and Olustee to their masters to conciliate the South," he told visitors to the White House in 1864, but "I should be damned in time and in eternity for so doing. The world shall know that I will keep my faith to friends and enemies, come what will."[29]

As time went on, Lincoln grew steadily more confident that he had made the right decision. He worried less about how the proclamation might fare in a courtroom, confident that his notion of emancipation as a valid exercise of his powers as commander in chief would withstand legal scrutiny.[30] While he privately sometimes expressed an interest in both compensating slaveholders and enacting some sort of voluntary colonization scheme, those expressions became steadily more sporadic.[31] He was far more emphatic in his insistence that emancipation was an accomplished fact, that his legacy rested upon his giving of freedom to the slaves, and that all Americans, particularly white Southerners, must make their peace with the new way of things.

THE WAR AND AFRICAN AMERICANS

L incoln absolutely had to maintain that the Confederacy was a legal and constitutional nonentity. To do otherwise would have undermined his justification for the war. Recognizing the Confederacy's legitimacy by definition would have shattered Lincoln's argument that the American Union was perpetual and unbreakable; he would have had no reasonable justification for invading the South if the South had indeed become a genuine sovereign nation. Nor could he have effectively blocked efforts by European nations like England and France to afford formal diplomatic recognition to the Confederacy.

Certain troubling implications followed from this line of thought, however. If Confederates were merely rebellious American citizens, then they might possess at least some standing in an American court of law. And if the Confederates were simply rebellious Americans, then the only real legal recourse open to the Lincoln administration by way of punishment was to try them for treason. But this opened a Pandora's box of problems.

Article III, Section 3 defines treason as "consist[ing] only in levying War against them, or in adhering to their Enemies, giving them Aid and Comfort." It further stipulates that "No Person shall be convicted of Treason unless on the Testimony of two Witnesses to the same overt Act, or on Confession in open Court." Section 3 brims with limitations and qualifiers: Treason is "only" a certain narrowly defined offense, conviction requires two witnesses, and the illegal act must be "overt." The clause is a striking exception to the Framers' normally broad and open-ended approach to constitutional language. The Framers wanted Americans to have the liberty to engage in political dissent without the threat of a treason trial hanging constantly over their heads, so they required treason to meet the test of being an "overt" act, and they set a high evidentiary bar by requiring two courtroom witnesses to the deed. Treason trials as a result are extremely rare in American history. Very early on, the US Supreme Court interpreted the Constitution's treason provisions narrowly and purposely made the government's task in bringing a treason indictment difficult.[1]

Lincoln occasionally referenced the rebellion as an act of "treason" and the Confederates as "traitors" (though less often than one might think).[2] But this had nothing to do with the legal and constitutional realities of the situation. The Lincoln administration did not want to face the daunting prospect of actually bringing treason charges against rebels. The Constitution set the bar for conviction too high, and the president did not want a treason conviction overturned by the same Supreme Court that gave him *Ex Parte Merryman*. Lincoln also would not have wanted to give Confederates and their sympathizers the stage of a treason trial on which they could display their arguments that secession was constitutional—arguments that might actually sound plausible to some who heard them. One of the more remarkable features of the American Civil War was that, in this penultimate act of rebellion, no Confederate from Jefferson Davis on down was tried for treason.[3]

In practical terms, the Lincoln administration had to treat Confederates as though they were citizens of a de facto foreign nation, even as Lincoln himself vigorously denied such a nation existed. When Confederate soldiers were captured in battle, for example, they were not jailed as criminals and pirates, and no serious thought was given to leveling indictments against them as such. They were either exchanged or placed in prisoner-of-war camps, exactly as if they were soldiers fighting for a foreign nation. Nor did Lincoln show interest in branding Confederate sympathizers "traitors"; when local officials (particularly in the Border States) tried to bring treason charges against Confederate sympathizers in their midst, the Lincoln administration allowed those indictments to lie dormant until local courts eventually dropped them entirely.[4]

Depending upon the situation, Confederates both were and were not traitors. They both were and were not American citizens, and they both were and were not alien enemy combatants. It was only a matter of time before this anomalous situation found its way into a courtroom, and it did so via yet another legally ambivalent dimension of the Northern war effort: the blockade.

Lincoln officially proclaimed a Northern naval blockade of the Confederate coast in April 1861. Soon thereafter, the Union navy as part of its normal operations seized four ships and their cargos as blockade prizes, claiming the vessels were doing business with the Confederacy. The owners sued the federal government, attacking not just Lincoln's decision to create such a blockade, but also his overall powers as commander in chief. Pointing out that Congress had never formally declared war against the Confederacy, they wondered how any state of war could exist at all, merely upon the president's word; and if no actual war existed, then their clients' cargo could not legally be seized. If successful, their argument could have seriously impeded not only the blockade, but many of the Lincoln administration's policies.

The Supreme Court's decision in what came to be known as the *Prize* cases was the court's most important ruling of the war, the only opportunity for the nation's highest tribunal to judge the constitutionality of the war itself. After nearly two years of litigation in the lower federal courts, a closely divided court handed down its decision in March 1863. A majority of five justices upheld the government's seizure of the four vessels and validated the Lincoln administration's approach to the war. Pointing out that "a civil war is never solemnly declared," they deemed unreasonable the suggestion that Congress must formally declare via its Article I, Section 8 in order for a state of war to legally exist. "As a civil war is never publicly proclaimed . . . its actual existence is a fact in our domestic history which the Court is bound to notice and to know."

This being the case, the court pointed out that civil wars sometimes required the government to treat insurgents as rebellious citizens, while on other occasions the two sides dealt with each other as belligerents. The president's primary duty was to fulfill his constitutional oath and defend the nation; and if this required him to treat the Rebels as de facto foreign enemies (without recognizing the legitimacy of their cause), then so be it. "It is not necessary that the independence of the revolted province or State be acknowledged in order to constitute it a party belligerent in a war according to the law of nations," the court ruled.

As commander in chief, Lincoln was in the best position to know what was necessary to secure victory. The court respected the president's judgment in this regard: "He must determine what degree of force the crisis demands." "Whether the President, in fulfilling his duties as commander in chief in suppressing an insurrection, has met with such armed hostile resistance and a civil war of such alarming proportions as will compel him to accord to them the character of belligerents is a question to be decided by him," the judges believed, "and this Court must be governed by the decisions and acts of the political department of the Government to which this power was entrusted." In essence the court ruled that the government could have it both ways: A Confederate could be defined as either an alien combatant fighting on behalf of a de facto nation, or a rebellious American citizen, depending upon which approach was best suited to producing a Union victory.

Lincoln got what he needed to continue fighting the war on his terms. The *Prize* cases gave Lincoln the flexibility he needed to prosecute the war by defining the status of Confederates as both rebellious citizens and alien combatants. The decision "resolved a great doubt that had been hanging over the administration's war effort and immensely strengthened the hand of those who were struggling to preserve the Union," argues historian Brian McGinty.[5]

But what about the other great citizenship question: What about African Americans and their citizenship status, or perhaps lack thereof? Emancipation had opened up an entirely new set of questions about the nature of American citizenship. After 1863 African Americans were no longer recognized by the American legal system as property. But were they full-blown citizens? If so, what did that mean, exactly?

At bottom, the constitutional question was one of federal author-ity. Most African Americans lived in Southern states controlled by whites who, whatever the war's outcome, could not be expected to extend any sort of citizenship rights to the black people living within their borders. Northern states weren't much inclined to do so, either. If the federal government stood by and did nothing—pretty much its position on citizenship since the nation's founding—then eman-cipation would mean only an absence of slavery; it would guarantee African Americans nothing else at all.

The federal government began to take baby steps in the direction of creating nationally sanctioned citizenship rights after it embraced emancipation as its official policy. Attorney General Bates issued an opinion in November 1862—the period between the preliminary proclamation and the final Emancipation Proclamation—affirm-ing the fact of African American citizenship, while at the same time denying that citizenship must include a right to vote or hold office. "The Constitution of the United States does not declare who are and who are not citizens, nor does it attempt to describe the constituent elements of citizenship," Bates pointed out. "It leaves that quality where it found it, resting upon the fact of home-birth, and upon the laws of the several States." That said, however, Bates rejected the very core of Taney's *Dred Scott* ruling. "It is strenuously insisted by some," Bates wrote, with a pointed reference to Taney, "that 'persons of color,' though born in the country, are not capable of being citi-zens of the United States. . . . The exclusion, if it exists, must then rest upon some fundamental fact which, in the reason and nature of things, is so inconsistent with citizenship that the two cannot coexist in the same person. Is mere color such a fact? Let those who assert it prove that it is so. It has never been so understood." Bates's opinion here was not a statement that the federal government had a positive duty to protect the citizenship status of African Americans; rather, it was more concerned with simply stating that neither Roger Taney nor anyone else could read blacks out of the national body politic via the US Constitution.[6]

In the months following his Emancipation Proclamation, Lin-coln remained silent on these issues. Charles Sumner groused about

Lincoln's lack of assistance when Sumner spearheaded attempts to end racial discrimination in Washington, DC (one area where Congress possessed indisputable authority)—writing that Lincoln "does not know how to help or is not moved to help. For instance, I do not remember that I have had help from him in any of the questions which I have conducted—although a word from him in certain quarters would have saved me much trouble."[7]

But Lincoln did sign into law the reforms passed by Congress without objection. As a general rule, his relations with Congress were amiable and cooperative, even with the Radicals, who possessed prickly personalities and a jaundiced view of the president's job performance. They are "the unhandiest devils in the world to deal with," Lincoln sighed, "but after all their faces are set Zionwards."[8]

They were like a stormy marriage, Lincoln and the Radicals: long periods of harmony punctuated with occasional squabbles, some loud enough for the neighbors to hear—but without any lasting damage, and with a general realization on both sides that everyone involved had their hearts in the right place. One area sparked serious tension between Lincoln and Congress, however, which increased as the war progressed and Union victory seemed certain: Reconstruction.

Fighting a large-scale civil war had been ambiguous enough as a matter of American constitutionalism, given the gray areas and untested aspects of the Constitution's various war-making provisions. But Reconstruction was even more problematic, because the Constitution offered practically no guidance concerning how rebellious American states could be reintegrated back into the Union. Few of the Founding Fathers could have foreseen secession, and fewer still could have envisioned the need to put the Union back together again, let alone design a clear constitutional mechanism for doing so.

The Reconstruction question plaguing the government was perhaps the most basic constitutional issue of all: Which branch was primarily responsible for creating Reconstruction policies? Arguably this was the president's call, a natural outgrowth of his war-making authority. The war was giving the government something to reconstruct, and anything involving a war put Lincoln as commander in chief at the head of the decision-making line.

But Reconstruction might just as plausibly fall within the purview of Congress, since Reconstruction also involved setting rules and guidelines after the shooting stopped. Many congressmen looked to the "guarantee clause" in Article IV, Section 4 of the Constitution, which called upon the federal government to guarantee a "Republican form of Government" for all the States in the Union, as a mandate for their active involvement in Reconstruction. Reading "Republican" as a form of representative democracy, they reasoned that the slave-holding Southern states had most assuredly not given a republican form of government to their African American citizens, and it was subsequently Congress's duty to see that they did so.

These were Lincoln's fellow Republicans who were making such arguments. But presidents have had a strong tendency throughout American history to jealously guard the prerogatives of the executive branch, party affiliation and other political considerations be damned—and Lincoln was no exception. Republicans in Congress very badly wanted a strong, perhaps even controlling voice in Reconstruction policy making. But Lincoln felt just as strongly that Reconstruction was primarily a presidential matter, and he was determined to assert his power in this key area of government policy making. "I had considerable talk with the President this evening on this subject," John Hay wrote in his diary on July 31, 1863. "He considers it the greatest question ever presented to practical statesmanship."[9]

Five months later, Lincoln issued a formal Proclamation of Amnesty and Reconstruction." In it he laid out what amounted to a first draft of a presidential Reconstruction plan. His plan contained essentially two parts: first, a requirement that at least 10 percent of the qualified voters of 1860 in a given state take an oath of loyalty to the Union; and second, that these voters create a new state government, which would be both broadly "republican" in form (citing Article IV, Section 4), and would bestow permanent freedom upon any slaves residing within their borders. Lincoln also indicated, in a rather vague way, that he would not object if a state saw fit to "provide for their education . . . as a temporary arrangement, with their present condition as a laboring, landless, and homeless class."[10]

Lincoln did not moor his authority to propose such a plan in his power as commander in chief; in fact, he did not mention his war-making authority in the proclamation at all. Instead, he fastened upon another clause in Article II, Section 2's bestowal upon the president the "Power to Grant Reprieves and Pardons for Offenses against the United States, except in Cases of Impeachment." Lincoln mentioned this pardoning power in the very first sentence of his proclamation, as the primary constitutional foundation for his Reconstruction authority, and then he referenced it again three more times for good measure.

Lincoln was acting the part of a shrewd lawyer here. He knew that his war-making powers gave him great influence and control over government policy only while the fighting continued. But the pardoning power . . . now *that* was a truly powerful legal tool. It was nearly unlimited and could not be gainsaid by either Congress or the courts. "The Constitution authorizes the Executive to grant or withhold the pardon at his own absolute discretion," he pointed out to Congress in his 1863 annual address. Congress itself had reinforced the president's pardoning role in Section 13 of the Second Confiscation Act, where it stated that "the President is hereby authorized, at any time hereafter, by proclamation, to extend to persons who may have participated in the existing rebellion in any State or part thereof, pardon and amnesty, with such exceptions and at such time and on such conditions as he may deem expedient for the public welfare." Lincoln made it a point to quote this section of the Second Confiscation Act in his Reconstruction proclamation.[11]

On the face of it, Lincoln's proclamation—dubbed the "Ten Percent Plan" by the press—was remarkably mild. It was forgiving in its treatment of former Confederates, exempting from the oath only high-ranking members of the Confederate government and military service, and "all who have engaged in any way in treating colored persons or white persons, in charge of such, otherwise than lawfully as prisoners of war."[12] It said nothing about granting African Americans basic citizenship rights such as trial procedures, the suffrage, or other political activities, nor did it offer any solution to the problem of defining a national set of citizenship rights to be protected by the federal government—the Radicals' sine qua non for any serious Reconstruction plan. Apparently the president was content to allow the states to continue regulating most areas of civic life, including most aspects of citizenship.

On the other hand, Lincoln's plan did tie Reconstruction directly to emancipation. He had now clarified that the institution of slavery was irrevocably dead and buried. Human bondage had no future in the newly reconstructed United States, and American citizenship did not include (as Roger Taney had asserted in *Dred Scott*) the sacred right to own another human being. This was no small achievement.

But the Ten Percent Plan created trepidation among Radicals, not only because many disagreed with the president's relatively mild approach, but also because it seemed to them that, if Congress passively accepted the Ten Percent Plan without question or modification, they would in effect cede to the executive branch control of Reconstruction policy. Accordingly, the Radical leadership in Congress drafted its own Reconstruction plan, which passed both houses and landed on the president's desk for his signature in July 1864. Named the Wade-Davis Bill after its sponsors (Benjamin Wade of Ohio and Henry Winter Davis of Maryland), the plan was a far more stern blueprint for Reconstruction than the president's plan. Where Lincoln required only 10 percent of the registered voters of 1860 to take an oath of loyalty to the Union, the Wade-Davis plan required a majority of a given state's population to do so. And their oath was not—as with Lincoln—an affirmation of future loyalty to the United States; rather, it required an affirmation that the oath-taker had never been disloyal to the Union. This last provision, the so-called "iron clad oath," was obviously aimed at bestowing citizenship status upon African Americans, for who else realistically among Southerners could take such an oath?

The Wade-Davis Bill was rooted in the guarantee clause, a source of constitutional authority that Lincoln and Congress alike referenced. Both could do so with equal validity, since Article IV did not specify which branch of the federal government was responsible for guaranteeing a republican form of government. But Congress sought the higher ground here, including in the Wade-Davis Bill micromanaged orders to the president concerning exactly how he was to administer the reconstructed states, even down to how much a state's provisional governor should be paid. The bill also made it quite clear that the president answered to Congress, and not vice versa. He could appoint the provisional governors only with the advice and consent of the Senate, and he could certify that a state had achieved a "republican form of government" only with prior congressional approval.[13]

Adding a further affront, Congress did not send the bill to the White House for Lincoln's signature until the very end of their session, giving him almost no time to properly peruse its contents, or think through its ramifications. Lincoln responded with a so-called "pocket veto." He allowed the congressional session (and the Wade-Davis Bill) to expire without his signature, killing the bill. He followed the pocket veto with a carefully worded, rather cagey public message. He stated that he had allowed the Wade-Davis Bill to expire due primarily to the short length of time he was given, and that he was not "inflexibly committed to any single plan of restoration." He also suggested that he was not necessarily opposed to the Wade-Davis approach "as one very proper plan for the loyal people of any State choosing to adopt it."[14]

Behind the scenes, Lincoln—while genuinely anxious about the last-minute delivery of the bill to his desk, which he complained was "a matter of too much importance to be swallowed in that way"— actually did have time to analyze the constitutional implications of the Wade-Davis Bill. He did not like what he saw. The Wade-Davis approach rested upon multiple, highly dubious constitutional proposals in Lincoln's eyes.[15]

First, he was bothered by the implication contained in the plan that Congress could step in and order any state to abolish slavery. Lincoln's interpretation of the Constitution in this regard had always been narrowly focused: Only the president could abolish slavery, and he could do so only through his war powers. "I conceive that I may in an emergency do things on military grounds which cannot be done constitutionally by Congress," he told Zachariah Chandler, who visited Lincoln's office during the waning moments of the congressional session, urging Lincoln to sign the Wade-Davis Bill. "I do not see how any of us now can deny and contradict all we have always said, that congress has no constitutional power over slavery in the states."[16]

Second (and perhaps most importantly) the Wade-Davis Bill compromised the premise that Lincoln had maintained from the very outset of the war—that the rebellious Confederate states never actually left the Union. Wade-Davis was founded upon the Radicals' "state suicide" theory, the only constitutional theory that would allow Congress to dictate such Reconstruction terms. Lincoln found this approach both inappropriate and dangerous. Wade-Davis "seems to me to make the fatal admission . . . that states whenever they please may of their own motion dissolve their connection with the Union," he told Chandler. "Now we cannot survive that admission I am convinced. If that be true I am not President [and] these gentlemen are not Congress." The whole argument about whether or not a seceded state had or had not committed constitutional suicide, Lincoln believed, was mischievous, "a merely metaphysical question and one unnecessary to be forced into discussion," as he thought the Wade-Davis approach would surely do.[17]

Lincoln pocket-vetoed the bill for reasons that were far more momentous and complex than those he stated in his public explanation. He knew this too was fraught with peril, risking an open fight with powerful men in his own party. "If they choose to make a point upon this I do not doubt they can do me harm," he confessed to Hay.[18]

In constitutional terms, the Wade-Davis Bill was a powerful congressional shot across the bow at what some thought was unchecked presidential authority. Wade and Davis made this abundantly clear by issuing an acid public statement after the veto, accusing Lincoln of "a grave Executive usurpation" and declaring their intent to "check the encroachments of the Executive on the authority of Congress, and to require it to confine itself to its proper sphere." The president, they argued, should "obey and execute [and not] make the laws—to suppress by arms armed rebellion, and leave political reorganization to Congress." Many other congressmen were likewise incensed at the president. "The radicals, so called, are as virulent and bitter as ever," thought Noah Brooks, a California newspaper correspondent who was friendly towards the president, "and they have gladly seized upon this occasion to attempt to reorganize the faction which fought against Lincoln's nomination (in 1864). . . . [T]hey nose out 'Executive interference with legislative prerogatives,' [and] they discern conservative policy afar off."[19]

Some feared that Lincoln was contemplating broad amnesty for the Rebels, giving out free passes to Confederates via his pardoning power. But the Radicals misread their man if they thought Lincoln was preparing to distribute wholesale pardons to white ex-Confederates while leaving the former freedmen to twist in the wind (as Lincoln's successor Andrew Johnson would do, with disastrous results). Even as he nixed the Wade-Davis Bill, Lincoln quietly sent other signals that he was slowly but surely moving in the Radicals' direction. During the waning months of the war, as the Confederacy crumbled beneath the feet of the victorious Union armies, Lincoln began to sound quite a bit like a Republican Radical himself.

Near the top of the Radicals' wish list was suffrage. Giving African American men the power of the vote was a longstanding dream of antislavery activists. Trouble was, voting requirements had always fallen well within the scope of state powers, and very few states, even in the North, were much disposed towards granting black people this most cherished of American political rights. If Radical Republicans truly wanted to give African Americans the vote, they would have to effect something of a constitutional revolution, using federal power to hammer past reluctant state legislatures and directly impact individual lives. Here again was that selfsame controversy about the true locus of American citizenship.

Lincoln always believed, along with the vast majority of white Americans, that voting should remain a state matter; and before 1860 he was in no sense an advocate for African American suffrage.[20] But like many other Americans, he grew during the war. He heard the stories filtering up from the South of Union soldiers' encounters with the horrors of the slave system. He saw black men fight and die with valor in the Union army, which earned them his everlasting respect. By 1864, he began to at least imagine the idea of a mixed-race American community, one in which it was no longer so unthinkable that African Americans could participate in America's civic life.

Sometime in early 1864, Lincoln received a letter from James S. Wadsworth, a Union army general from New York who was politically well-connected in antislavery circles. Wadsworth suggested that Lincoln might strike a bargain with white Southerners: universal amnesty in exchange for universal suffrage—that is, voting rights for blacks and whites alike. Lincoln's reply was encouraging, if characteristically guarded: "I cannot see, if universal amnesty is granted, how, under the circumstances, I can avoid exacting in return universal suffrage, or, at least, suffrage on the basis of intelligence and military service." The president revealed the deep impression black soldiers had made on his thinking, as well as his understanding of his own role: "As the nation's guardian of these people, who have so heroically vindicated their manhood on the battle-field, where, in assisting to save the life of the Republic, they have demonstrated in blood their right to the ballot, which is but the humane protection of the flag they have so fearlessly defended."[21]

In March 1864, Lincoln took another quiet, low-key step in the direction of African American suffrage, this time in a letter to Michael Hahn, governor of the newly elected loyal administration in Union-occupied Louisiana. Mentioning the fact that a convention was about to meet in Louisiana that would draft a new state constitution, Lincoln wrote to Hahn, "I barely suggest for your private consideration, whether some of the colored people may not be let in—as, for instance, the very intelligent, and especially those who have fought gallantly in our ranks. They would probably help, in some trying time to come, to keep the jewel of liberty within the family of freedom." Lincoln emphasized that this was a suggestion only, in no sense an order, and he stressed his desire that Hahn keep their correspondence out of the public eye.[22]

The letters to Wadsworth and Hahn might not seem like much to modern Americans. Lincoln still conceptualized suffrage as primarily a state matter, and particularly in his letter to Hahn he sounded a note of suggestion and gentle persuasion, rather than any energetic resolve. It was also a futile gesture, because Louisiana's convention did nothing about granting the vote to African Americans.[23]

But this sort of quiet, behind-the-scenes, gently persuasive approach was not indicative of presidential weakness, or a lack of resolve. Lincoln was growing slowly but steadily bolder, his face "set Zionwards" in much the same general direction as the Radicals. As the war drew to a close, Lincoln redoubled his efforts in another, related area of black rights: the pursuit of a constitutional amendment abolishing slavery.

A bill calling for Congress to abolish slavery by amending the Constitution was first introduced in Congress in December 1863 and became the impetus for a number of proposed amendments in the ensuing months, some more limited in scope than others. Some in Congress did not want to amend the Constitution at all, worrying that in doing so they were upsetting the delicate constitutional mechanisms put in place by the Founding Fathers of 1787. More moderate Republicans and Democrats preferred an amendment that was narrowly tailored and designed only to end slavery, while Radicals wanted an amendment that would not only end slavery but offer some sort of guarantee of racial equality, which would have been a first step towards creating a nationally defined set of standards for American citizenship. Predictably enough, this touched off a firestorm of debate and controversy in Congress throughout much of 1864. A draft amendment passed the Senate but was rejected by the House in April.[24]

At first Lincoln took a hands-off approach to the amendment debates. Presidents during that era were reluctant to involve themselves too directly in congressional wrangling as a general thing, and the Constitution's Article V amendment clause gave the presidency no direct role in such proceedings. Still, Lincoln wanted an amendment abolishing slavery, particularly after his efforts to persuade individual states to adopt emancipation measures had borne so little fruit. He also had come to believe that a constitutional amendment would resolve the nagging "metaphysical question" concerning the seceded states' status in the Union. "It was to obviate this question [of "state suicide"] that I earnestly favored the movement of for an amendment to the Constitution abolishing slavery," he said. He also knew that a constitutional amendment would, once and for all, make his emancipation policy permanent and irrevocable.[25]

The failure of the amendment to clear the House was dismaying; and Lincoln worried so much about the project's fate that, in the fall of 1864, he took extraordinary pains to lobby individual congressman and press for its passage, "intervening more directly in the legislative process than at any other point in his presidency," according to historian Eric Foner. He called for ratification in his annual message to Congress, and he used his influence to ensure that a plank supporting ratification made its way into the Republican Party's 1864 election platform.[26]

Passage of the amendment was a momentous event in American constitutional history. Its supporters made it clear that they saw the measure as more than simply ending slavery in America. It established for the first time in American history a national government mandate to safeguard Americans' personal liberty against government encroachment on both the national and state level. "It is not enough to secure the death of Slavery throughout the Rebel and belligerent region only," Charles Sumner declared. "Slavery wherever it exists [is] not only a crime against humanity, but [is] a disturber of the public peace and spoiler of the public liberties, including liberty of the press, liberty of speech, and liberty of travel and transit. . . . [T]he defiant pretensions of the [slave] master . . . are in direct conflict with the paramount rights of the national government." For Sumner and other Radicals especially, the Thirteenth Amendment at least implied a national guarantee of basic citizenship rights.[27]

Whether or not Lincoln shared the Radicals' expansive reading of the amendment's language is unknown; in public he took the most conservative available approach, emphasizing the amendment's value to the ongoing project of ending the war and ensuring no future agitation over slavery would ever again disturb the American Union. When it was finally ratified by both houses of Congress on February 1, 1865, the president was very pleased. Responding to a serenade of well-wishers who appeared at the White House that evening, he enthused that "this amendment is a King's cure for all the evils" of the war: "it winds the whole thing up. . . . the fitting if not indispensable adjunct to the consummation of the great game we are playing."[28]

He was serenaded again a few weeks later, this time in response to the news of Lee's surrender at Appomattox. Reconstruction and the postwar future were very much on Lincoln's mind that evening, as were the various controversies surrounding the newly reconstructed loyal government in Louisiana. Realizing that not everyone was satisfied with the cautious approach he had taken in Louisiana, and in particular understanding that the battles over the Wade-Davis Bill and his Ten Percent Plan still rankled among many fellow Republicans, he urged patience in his speech to the crowd that evening. But then, and for the first time in such a public fashion, Lincoln signaled his support for African American suffrage. "It is also unsatisfactory to some that the elective franchise is not given to the colored man," he said, referring to the new Louisiana legislature's failure to act on his behind-the-scenes suggestion to Governor Hahn. "I would myself prefer that it were now conferred on the very intelligent, and on those who serve our cause as soldiers."[29]

A Radical Republican might not have been so terribly impressed with this, the first public endorsement of African American suffrage by an American president. But others in the audience were—and not necessarily in a good way. "That means nigger equality," John Wilkes Booth seethed to fellow conspirator David Herrold; "now, by God! I'll put him through."[30]

EPILOGUE

"I hope to stand firm enough not to go backward, and yet not go forward fast enough to wreck the country's cause," Lincoln wrote to Zachariah Chandler in November 1863. It was an apt summary of Lincoln's entire approach to the war, the presidency, and the American political and constitutional system within which he operated.[1]

Lincoln's desire to strike this fine balance between progress and prudence, between what he thought the country needed to do and what he thought it would tolerate, could make him seem vacillating and slow to Radicals and other Americans who wanted to see faster and more revolutionary changes. On the other hand, many moderate and conservative Americans saw him recklessly pursuing a sweeping agenda of revolutionary change affecting both North and South, particularly in the area of race relations—change for which the country was unprepared.

With characteristic insight, Frederick Douglass saw precisely what Lincoln was about. "Viewed from the genuine abolition ground, Mr. Lincoln seemed tardy, cold, dull, and indifferent," Douglass declared, "but measuring him by the sentiment of his country, a sentiment he was bound as a statesman to consult, he was swift, zealous, radical, and determined."[2]

Lincoln moved steadily towards the Radicals' way of thinking during the final months of the war. A sitting American president who publicly endorsed the idea of African American suffrage was no small matter, not in that day and age. Even in his more cautious moments—his Ten Percent Plan, and his pocket veto of the Wade-Davis Bill—Lincoln let it be known that he was open to compromise and negotiation, and that his actions regarding Reconstruction were merely the opening moves in what would be a long and laborious process.

He would have brought to the task a robust and broad constructionist constitutionalism. Ever since his early days as an Illinois politician promoting economic growth and development, he viewed the Constitution through an interpretive framework stressing an energetic and activist government. During the sectional crisis of the 1850s and the war, he continued to read the Constitution expansively and with an eye towards increasing the federal government's capacity to meet the many and complex crises it faced. He was no tyrant, as some have suggested; but he did believe the government, and the presidency in particular, must be allowed the power necessary to win the war and ensure the survival of the American Union.

If this trend in his thinking had persisted, Lincoln would likely have spent his second term slowly but steadily gravitating towards the Radical position in areas related to the freedmen and their civil rights. It is reasonable to speculate that he would have been generally supportive of the efforts by Congress to nationalize basic American citizenship rights in the Civil Rights Act of 1866 and the Fourteenth and Fifteenth Amendments. Lincoln also would surely have offered his continued support for the Freedmen's Bureau and its efforts to educate ex-slaves and prepare them properly to compete in a free labor market; and as commander in chief of the US Army, he would also have surely been far more willing than his successor, Andrew Johnson, to commit military resources towards protection of the freedmen from the depredations and violence of their more vengeful white neighbors.

Lincoln would not have been interested in completely upending the American constitutional system, a system that remained state-centered in many ways. Nor would he have been afforded many opportunities to do so, because in peacetime he would have lost his primary constitutional weapon: his war-making powers as commander in chief. He still would have retained command of the nation's armed forces, of course. But Americans began to almost completely dismantle the victorious and massive Union army and navy soon after the Confederates surrendered. Lincoln could not have prevented this, and he would have found himself forced to work with a much smaller military apparatus as he tried to keep the peace in the occupied South.

He also would have been confronted with the stark political and constitutional necessity of sharing authority with Congress. War gives American presidents constitutional power they do not normally possess in peacetime; and it affords both an unusually large infusion of public goodwill and extraordinary deference from the other branches of government, as Americans try hard to rally around the flag and support their commander in chief. This spirit of goodwill and cooperation does tend to fade as wars grind on, however; and the Civil War was no exception. Lincoln's sharpest clashes with Congress came after 1863; and it is difficult to imagine the many powerful and earnestly committed men in Congress—especially the Radicals—deferring to Lincoln's judgment once the fighting ended.

Lincoln would have been compelled to call upon all his personal and political resources as he essentially renegotiated the power-sharing relationship between the executive and legislative branches of government, as both tried to set Reconstruction policy. Given that the guarantee clause was the constitutional foundation of Reconstruction, and given that neither branch of the federal government was specifically charged with safeguarding a republican form of government in the South, Congress would have been well within its rights to argue for a policy-making presence at least equal to—if not greater than—the presidency.

The Supreme Court would also have had to reasserted itself. After following the trend of deference to the president in wartime, the justices during the Andrew Johnson and Ulysses S. Grant administrations pulled back from their wartime acquiescence to executive decision making, as well as federal authority generally. Beginning in 1866 with *Ex Parte Milligan* (in which the court restricted the government's power to try a suspected Confederate sympathizer by military rather than civilian law), the court handed down a series of rulings that limited the federal government's power to protect individual civil rights from state authorities. Despite the fact that he had placed several of the judges on the Supreme Court's bench himself, Lincoln might well have faced an indifferent or even openly hostile court, had he tried to expand either his power or that of the federal government.

Lincoln would therefore have confronted a very complex political, legal, and constitutional environment after the war. Still, he had the advantage of possessing not only a powerful sense of the Constitution's capacity for expansion and development, but also an equally powerful sense of the moral content, the right and the wrong of things, and the place this moral sense occupied in his constitutional thought. This perhaps is the greatest lesson we can take from Abraham Lincoln's approach to the Constitution. While he greatly valued and cherished both the Constitution and the rule of law it represented, it was always for him a means to a higher, greater moral end—some "apple of gold."

The "apple" changed and evolved as Lincoln himself changed and evolved. Early in his life, the moral center of his constitutionalism was his deep reverence for the Framers and the Revolutionary generation. During the 1850s, Lincoln placed the Declaration of Independence at the moral apex of his constitutional thought. When the war broke out, he turned the Union—a Union that, eventually, would have no place for slavery—into his apple of gold. As the war progressed, Lincoln made emancipation and some measure of civic equality for African Americans his constitutional moral centerpiece; and this provided the impetus for his gradual shift in the direction of Radical Republicanism.

Slaveholders and their allies held that the Constitution's various compromises with slavery were themselves morally absolute, not to be challenged by any new progress in Americans' moral sensibilities concerning slavery or race. During the war, many of the more conservative Americans in the North believed that the Constitution's limitations on federal power trumped the national community's ability to defend itself, or rid itself of the war's principal cause via emancipation. Stephen Douglas, Roger Taney, George McClellan . . . at some point all argued that the Constitution, in the limited and proscribed way they read the document, trumped all other considerations.

Lincoln thought otherwise. He saw the Constitution and the rule of law it represented as a vehicle designed to get Americans somewhere, someplace higher and better than where they had been: a more perfect Union.

ACKNOWLEDGMENTS

NOTES

BIBLIOGRAPHY

INDEX

ACKNOWLEDGMENTS

In any of my scholarly endeavors related to Abraham Lincoln or the constitutional history of the Civil War era, I owe a permanent debt of gratitude to Phillip S. Paludan, my mentor at the University of Kansas, and Harold M. Hyman, professor emeritus at Rice University. Both communicated to me their intense interest in the war, the life and times of Lincoln, and above all the central importance of the Constitution in understanding the American experience.

I have also been blessed with excellent colleagues and friends at Anderson University, in particular Dan Allen, Michael Frank, David Murphy, Jaye Rogers, and Joel Schrock, all fellow faculty in the university's department of history and political science. I have also greatly benefited from the services of the university's Nicholson Library, and particularly of Jill Branscum, who has always been ready, able, and willing to help me with my various (and sometimes arcane) interlibrary loan needs.

Sylvia Rodrigue has been a very patient, kind, and thorough editor, helping me steer this project to a successful completion. I also greatly benefited from the advice and expertise of Sara Gabbard and Richard Etulain, as well as two anonymous peer reviewers who helped rescue me from various oversights and errors (any that remain being my sole responsibility). More generally the editors and staff of Southern Illinois University Press have always been ready to assist me with whatever issues or questions have arisen during the course of writing this book; their professionalism is second to none.

My wife, Julie, has been (as always) wonderfully patient and supportive, listening to my endless ramblings about Abraham Lincoln with commendable fortitude. The value of her love to me is impossible to adequately express. My children, Nathan and Rachel, likewise tolerate Lincoln's occasional intrusions into their lives with good humor. Finally, I should thank our cat, Ella, who provided many a welcome respite from long hours of research and writing. Fortunately, the damage she wrought on the manuscript by occasionally lying across my computer keyboard and randomly pressing the keys was easily remedied.

NOTES

Prologue

1. Booth quote in Henry Clay Whitney, *Life of Lincoln: Lincoln, the President* (New York: Baker and Taylor, 1908), 2:322; the source of this quote is David E. Herold, Lincoln's coconspirator; Whitney was a friend and contemporary of Lincoln; there are variations on this quote; see e.g. Michael W. Kauffman, *American Brutus: John Wilkes Booth and the Lincoln Conspiracies* (New York: 2004), 210; and Michael E. Burlingame, *Lincoln: A Life* (Baltimore: Johns Hopkins University Press, 2010), 2:803; I have used Whitney's version, since he was a friend and contemporary of Lincoln, and his version is the closest chronologically to the actual event.

2. Lincoln, Last Public Address, Apr. 11, 1865, in Roy P. Basler, ed., *Collected Works of Abraham Lincoln* (hereinafter referred to as *CW*) (New Brunswick: Rutgers University Press, 1953), 8:399–405.

3. George Anastoplo, *Abraham Lincoln: A Constitutional Biography* (New York: Rowman and Littlefield, 2001); Daniel Farber, *Lincoln's Constitution* (Chicago: University of Chicago Press, 2003); George P. Fletcher, *Our Secret Constitution: How Lincoln Redefined American Democracy* (Cambridge: Oxford University Press, 2001).

4. Phillip S. Paludan, *The Presidency of Abraham Lincoln* (Lawrence: University Press of Kansas, 1994); Mark E. Neely Jr., *Last Best Hope of Earth: Abraham Lincoln and the Promise of America* (Cambridge: Harvard University Press, 1995); James M. McPherson, *Abraham Lincoln and the Second American Revolution* (Cambridge: Oxford University Press, 1992).

5. See for example essays by Frank J. Williams, James Oakes, and Herman Belz, in Joseph R. Fornieri and Sara Vaughn Gabbard, eds., *Lincoln's America, 1809–1865* (Carbondale: Southern Illinois University Press, 2008); essays by Mark Neely, James Oakes, and Michael Vorenberg in Eric Foner, ed., *Our Lincoln: New Perspectives on Lincoln and His World* (New York: W. W. Norton, 2008); essays by Phillip Paludan and William E. Gienapp in James M. McPherson, ed., *"We Cannot Escape History": Lincoln and Last Best Hope of Earth* (Urbana: University of Illinois Press, 1995).

6. Text of Speech at <http://www.thurgoodmarshall.com/speeches/constitutional_speech.htm>, accessed Dec. 9, 2010.

7. Lincoln, Address on Colonization to a Deputation of Negroes, Aug. 14, 1862, *CW* 5:372–73; Lincoln to Joshua Speed, Aug. 24, 1855, *CW* 2:320.

8. Hendrik Hartog, "The Constitution of Aspiration and 'The Rights That Belong to Us All,'" *Journal of American History* 74 (Dec. 1987): 1013.

1. The Constitution in Lincoln's Early Years

1. Nathaniel Grigsby, Silas Richardson, Nancy Richardson, and John Romine, interview with William H. Herndon, Sept. 14, 1865, in Douglas L. Wilson and Rodney O. Davis, eds., *Herndon's Informants: Letters, Interviews, and Statements about Abraham Lincoln* (hereinafter referred to as *HI*) (Urbana: University of Illinois Press, 1997), 118.

2. On this point, see Robert Bray's excellent treatment of Lincoln's early reading habits in his perceptive and thorough study *Reading with Lincoln* (Carbondale: Southern Illinois University Press, 2010), esp. 41–80.

3. Lincoln, Speech before the Springfield Washington Temperance Society, Feb. 22, 1842, *CW* 1:279.

4. Lincoln, Address to the Young Men's Lyceum of Springfield, Illinois, Jan. 27, 1838, *CW* 1:112.

5. For a good general overview of Washington in American memory, see Richard Brookhiser, *Founding Father: Rediscovering George Washington* (New York: Free Press, 1997), esp. 159–85.

6. Lincoln, brief autobiography, June 15, 1858, *CW* 2:459; Lincoln, autobiography for John L. Scripps, c. June 1860, *CW* 4:65; there are many fine studies of Lincoln's early years in Illinois; see e.g. Kenneth J. Winkle, *Young Eagle: The Rise of Abraham Lincoln* (New York: Taylor, 2001), chaps. 1–3; Douglas L. Wilson, *Honor's Voice: The Transformation of Abraham Lincoln* (New York: Vintage, 1999); and Benjamin P. Thomas's older but still valuable *Lincoln's New Salem* 2nd ed. (Carbondale: Southern Illinois University Press, 1988).

7. Jason Duncan to William H. Herndon, c. 1866–1867, *HI* 540–41; Burlingame, *Lincoln: A Life*, 1:81–87, offers a nice summary of Green's influence on Lincoln.

8. Mentor Graham, interview with William H. Herndon, May 29, 1865, *HI* 9; Lynn McNulty Greene to William H. Herndon, July 30, 1865, *HI* 81; and Jason Duncan to William H. Herndon, c. 1866–1867, *HI* 541; Russell Godbey, interview with William H. Herndon, c. 1865–1866, *HI* 450.

9. Sir William Blackstone, *Commentaries on the Laws of England, in Four Books*, 13th ed. (London: A Strahan, 1800), 1:8; it is not known precisely which edition of Blackstone Lincoln owned and studied.

10. Lincoln to Usher F. Linder, Feb. 20, 1848, *CW* 1:454.

11. Lincoln, Notes for a Law Lecture, c. July 1850, *CW* 2:81.

12. Lincoln, "Communication to the People of Sangamon County," Mar. 9, 1832, *CW* 1:5–9.

13. Hamilton, Opinion as to the Constitutionality of a National Bank, 1791; <http://avalon.law.yale.edu/18th_century/bank-ah.asp>, accessed Oct. 22, 2009.

14. Thomas Jefferson, Opinion as to the Constitutionality of the National Bank, 1791; <http://avalon.law.yale.edu/18th_century/bank-tj.asp>, accessed Oct. 22, 2009; see also David N. Mayer, *The Constitutional Thought of Thomas Jefferson* (Charlottesville: University of Virginia Press, 1995).

15. "Lincoln, Speech on the Sub-Treasury, December 26, 1839, CW 1:171.

16. Lincoln, Speech at Cincinnati, Ohio, Sept. 17, 1859, *CW* 3:459; on Lincoln's various dealings with entrepreneurs in his legal practice, see Dirck, *Lincoln the Lawyer*, 76–98.

17. Lincoln, Address to the Young Men's Lyceum of Springfield, Jan. 27, 1838, *CW* 1:114.

18. Lincoln, Speech in Worcester, Massachusetts, Sept. 12, 1848, *CW* 2:3; Lincoln, fragment on Slavery, c. Apr. 1854, *CW* 2:222 (emphasis in original); Lincoln, Speech in Chicago, Illinois, July 10, 1858, *CW* 2:484; there are of course many studies that address Lincoln's attitude towards slavery; the best recent treatment is Eric Foner, *The Fiery Trial: Abraham Lincoln and American Slavery* (New York: W. W. Norton, 2010); also useful is Richard Striner's extremely positive analysis of Lincoln in *Father Abraham: Lincoln's Relentless Struggle to End Slavery* (Cambridge: Oxford University Press, 2007); George M. Fredrickson's more balanced study that focuses on race and slavery, *Big Enough to Be Inconsistent: Abraham Lincoln Confronts Slavery and Race* (Cambridge: Harvard University Press, 2008); of the many essays that treat the subject, quite useful on Lincoln's prewar attitudes about race and slavery are Michael Burlingame's "'I Used to Be a Slave': The Origins of Lincoln's Hatred of Slavery," in his *The Inner World of Abraham Lincoln* (Urbana: University of Illinois Press, 1997), 20–56; James Oakes, "Natural Rights, Citizenship Rights, States Rights, and Black Rights: Another Look at Lincoln and Race," in James M. McPherson, ed., *Our Lincoln: New Perspectives on Lincoln and His World* (New York: W. W. Norton, 2009), 109–34; Kenneth J. Winkle, "'Paradox Though It May Seem': Lincoln on Antislavery, Race, and the Union, 1837–1860," in Brian R. Dirck, ed., *Lincoln Emancipated: The President and the Politics of Race* (Carbondale: Southern Illinois University Press, 2007), 8–28.

19. Lincoln quoted in Donald E. and Virginia Fehrenbacher, eds., *Recollected Words of Abraham Lincoln* (Stanford, 1996), 61.

20. Protest in Illinois Legislature over Slavery, Mar. 3, 1837, *CW* 1:75.

21. William M. Wiecek, *The Sources of Antislavery Constitutionalism* (Ithaca: Cornell University Press, 1977).

22. Lysander Spooner, *The Unconstitutionality of Slavery* (New York: Burt Franklin, 1860), 9; see also Wiecek, *The Sources of Antislavery Constitutionalism*, chaps. 3–4.

23. Kentucky Resolutions, 1799; text from Avalon Project, Yale Law School, at <http://avalon.law.yale.edu/18th_century/kenres.asp>, accessed Dec. 18, 2009.

24. On the Bank War and currency issues, see Robert V. Remini, *Andrew Jackson and the Bank War*, 2nd ed., (New York: W. W. Norton, 1967); Lincoln's point of view on this issue is ably analyzed by Gabor Boritt in *Lincoln and the Economics of the American Dream*, chaps. 2–3.

25. Protest in Illinois Legislature on Slavery, Mar. 3, 1837, *CW* 1:75, fn2.

26. Executive Committee of the American Anti-slavery Society, *Slavery and the Internal Slave Trade in the United States of North America* (London: Thomas Ward, 1841), 205.

27. See Stanley Harrold, *Subversives: Antislavery Community in Washington, DC, 1828–1865* (Baton Rouge: Louisiana State University Press, 2003).

28. Executive Committee, *Slavery and the Internal Slave Trade*, 208.

29. Protest in Illinois Legislature on Slavery, Mar. 3, 1837, *CW* 1:75.

30. Lincoln, Eulogy on Henry Clay, July 6, 1852, *CW* 2:130.

2. Lincoln, the Constitution, and Slavery during the Sectional Crisis

1. Lincoln, Speech at Chicago, Illinois, July 10, 1858, *CW* 2:491.

2. "Celebrated" quote in James Washington Sheahan, *The Life of Stephen A. Douglas* (New York: Harper and Brothers, 1860), 187; 'hell of a storm" quote in Allen C. Guelzo, *Lincoln and Douglas: The Debates That Defined America* (New York: Simon and Schuster, 2008), 17.

3. Text of the Northwest Ordinance at <http://avalon.law.yale.edu/18th_century/nworder.asp>, accessed Jan. 11, 2010.

4. No author given, "The Missouri Question," in *The Panoplist, and Missionary Herald, for the Year 1820* (Boston: Samuel T. Armstrong, 1820), 67.

5. Lincoln quote from his eulogy on Henry Clay, July 6, 1852, *CW* 2:129; *Patriot* quoted in Glover Moore, *The Missouri Controversy, 1819–1821*, (Lexington: University of Kentucky Press, 1953), 244; on Clay's role in brokering the compromise, see Robert W. Remini, *Henry Clay: Statesman for the Union* (New York: W. W. Norton, 1991), 182–85.

6. Robert Pierce Forbes, *The Missouri Compromise and Its Aftermath: Slavery and the Meaning of America* (Chapel Hill: University of North Carolina Press, 2007), 6.

7. "Sacred thing" quote in Lincoln, Speech at Bloomington, Illinois, Sept. 26, 1854, *CW* 2:236.

8. Allen Johnson, *Stephen Douglas: A Study in American Politics* (New York: Macmillan, 1908), 271.

9. John Quincy Adams, *Memoirs of John Quincy* Adams (Philadelphia: J. P. Lippincott, 1877), 12:11; and Johannsen, *Douglas*, 133–35.

10. Adams, *Memoirs of John Quincy Adams*, 11:434.

11. On the Compromise of 1850, see generally Michael F. Holt, *The Political Crises of the 1850s* (New York: W. W. Norton, 1983); Holman Hamilton, *Prologue to Conflict: The Crisis and Compromise of 1850*, 2nd ed. (Lexington: University of Kentucky Press, 2005); and Potter, *Impending Crisis*, chap. 5.

12. Fillmore and Douglas quoted in Potter, *Impending Crisis*, 121.

13. Jefferson Davis, *Rise and Fall of the Confederate Government*, 1:28.

14. Johannsen, *Douglas*, 298.

15. Cass quoted in Hamilton, *Prologue to Conflict*, 145.

16. Ingersoll quote in *Appendix to the Congressional Globe, for the Second Session, Thirty-Third Congress* (Washington, DC: John C. Rives, 1855), 31:34.

17. Lincoln to George W. Rives, May 7, 1849, *CW* 2:46; see also Herndon, *Herndon's Lincoln*, chaps. 12–14.

18. Herndon, *Herndon's Lincoln*, 193; Lincoln to Jesse W. Fell, Enclosing Autobiography, Dec. 20, 1859 *CW* 3:512.

19. Herndon, *Herndon's Lincoln*, 225–26; Lincoln, Speech at Peoria, Illinois, Oct. 16, 1854, *CW* 2:282.

20. Lincoln, Speech in Bloomington, Illinois, Sept. 26, 1854, *CW* 2:238.

21. Lincoln, Speech in Springfield, Illinois, Oct. 4, 1854, *CW* 2:246.

22. *CW* 2:245.

23. Lincoln, Speech at Peoria, Illinois, Oct. 15, 1854, *CW* 3:255.

24. On this point, see William Weicek, *The Sources of Antislavery Constitutionalism* (Ithaca: Cornell University Press, 1977).

25. Lincoln, Speech in Springfield, Illinois, June 26, 1857, *CW* 2:404.

26. Lincoln, Eulogy of Henry Clay, July 6, 1852, *CW* 2:130; Speech in Petersburg, Illinois, Aug. 30, 1856, *CW* 2:368; Lincoln used the "self-evident lie" line in numerous anti-Nebraska speeches; see e.g. Speech at Chicago, Illinois, Oct. 27, 1854, *CW* 2:283.

27. Lincoln, Speech in Springfield, Illinois, Oct. 4, 1854, *CW* 2:245; Speech in Chicago, Illinois, Oct. 27, 1854, *CW* 2:284.

28. Lincoln, Speech in Springfield, Illinois, Oct. 4, 1854, *CW* 2:241; see also Speech in Peoria, Illinois, Oct. 16, 1854, *CW* 2:249.

29. Lincoln, Speech in Peoria, Illinois, Oct. 16, 1854, *CW* 2:276; for a similar use of the Declaration, see Lincoln's Speech at a Republican banquet, Chicago, Illinois, Dec. 10, 1856, *CW* 2:385.

30. Lincoln, Speech in Peoria, Illinois, Oct. 16, 1854, *CW* 2:266.

31. Lincoln, Fragment on the Constitution and the Union, c. Jan. 1861, *CW* 4:168–69.

32. See *CW* 4:168–69, fn 1.

3. Lincoln and the Declaration of Independence

1. Text of the 1856 Republican Party platform from <www.ushistory.org/gop/convention_1856republicanplatform.htm>; see also Eric Foner, *Free Soil, Free Labor, Free Men: The Ideology of the Republican Party Before the Civil War*, 2nd ed. (Oxford: Oxford University Press, 1995).

2. Boston *Atlas and Daily Bee*, July 22, 1858, quoted in Foner, *Free Soil, Free Labor, Free Men*, 207–8.

3. "Lincoln, Speech at Monticello, Illinois, July 29, 1858: CW 2:528; on the racial underpinnings of the early Republican Party, see James D. Bilotta, *Race and the Rise of the Republican Party, 1848–1865* (New York: Peter Lang, 1992).

4. Michael W. Cluskey, ed., *The Political Textbook, or Encyclopedia, Containing Everything Necessary for the Reference of the Politicians and Statesmen of the United States*, 2nd ed. (Philadelphia: James B. Smith, 1858), 618.

5. Joseph Gales, et al., eds., *Register of the Debates in Congress, Comprising the Leading Debates and Incidents of the Twentieth Congress* (Washington, DC: Gales and Eaton, 1828), 4:940; Keitt quote in Cluskey, ed., *The Political Textbook*, 604.

6. The best study of the *Dred Scott* case remains Don Fehrenbacher's magisterial *The* Dred Scott *Case: Its Significance in Law and Politics* (New York: Oxford University Press, 1978); also useful is R. Kent Newmyer, *The Supreme Court under Marshall and Taney*, 2nd ed. (New York: Harlan Davidson, 2006).

7. "Blot" quote in John Wesley, *Views of American Slavery, Taken a Century Ago* (Philadelphia: Assoc. of Friends, 1858), 138; James V. Marshall, *The United States Manual of Biography and History* (Philadelphia: James B. Smith, 1856), 434; Sara Mytton Maury, *The Statesmen of America in 1846* (Philadelphia: Carey and Hart, 1846), 88.

8. Samuel Tyler and Roger B. Taney, *Memoir of Roger Brooke Taney, LLD*, (Baltimore: John Murphy, 1872), 402; Don E. Fehrenbacher, Dred Scott *Case*, 560.

9. *Dred Scott v. Sandford*, 60 US 393 (1856); text of case taken from <http://laws.findlaw.com/us/60/393.html>, accessed Mar. 8, 2010.

10. Ibid.

11. John S. C. Abbott, *South and North; or, Impressions Received during a Trip to Cuba and the South* (New York: Abbey and Abbott, 1860), 159; Israel Washburn, *The Issues: The* Dred Scott *Decision: The Parties. Speech of Hon. Israel Washburn, Jun., of Maine, Delivered in the House of Representatives, May 19, 1860* (Washington, DC: Congressional Republican Committee, 1860), 7; [No author given] *Democratic Speeches On Kansas* (Washington, DC: Buell and Blanchard, 1856), 16; Frederick Milnes Edge, *Slavery Doomed; or, the Contest between Free and Slave Labor in the United States* (London: Smith, Elder, 1860), 156.

12. On Northerners' reaction to *Dred Scott*, see Fehrenbacher, Dred Scott *Case*, esp. 417–48.

13. Lincoln, Speech in Springfield, Illinois, June 26, 1857, *CW* 2:406.

14. On the historical development of judicial review, see Belz, *American Constitution: Origins and Development*, 1:156–77; and Larry D. Kramer, *The People Themselves: Popular Constitutionalism and Judicial Review* (Cambridge: Oxford University Press, 2005), chap. 2.

15. Lincoln, Speech in Springfield, Illinois, June 26, 1857, *CW* 2:401; see also his later Speech in Springfield, July 17, 1858, *CW* 2:516.

16. Lincoln, Speech in Springfield, Illinois, June 26, 1857, *CW* 2:401.

17. Lincoln, Speech in Chicago, Illinois, July 10, 1858, *CW* 2:495.

18. Lincoln, Speech in Chicago, Illinois, July 10, 1858, *CW* 2:495.

19. Douglas, *Speeches of Senator S. A. Douglas, On the Occasion of His Public Receptions by the People of New Orleans, Philadelphia, and Baltimore*, 7.

20. Second Debate, Freeport, Illinois, Aug. 27, 1858, *CW* 3:43.

21. *CW* 3:51–52.

22. Lincoln, Speech at Columbus, Ohio, Sept. 16, 1859, *CW* 3:417.

23. Potter, *Impending Crisis*, 336, 338; Potter is rightly critical of the time-bomb theory, as is James M. McPherson in his classic textbook on the era, *Ordeal by Fire: The Civil War and Reconstruction*, 108.

24. Lincoln to Henry Asbury, July 31, 1858, *CW* 2:530.

25. Douglas quoted in First Debate at Ottawa, Illinois, Aug. 21, 1858, *CW* 3:10.

26. Douglas quoted in Second Debate at Freeport, Illinois, Aug. 27, 1858, *CW* 3:56; on Illinois's antiblack laws, see Stephen Middleton, *The Black Laws of the Old Northwest: A Documentary History* (Westport: Greenwood Press, 1993).

27. Third Debate at Jonesboro, Illinois, Sept. 15, 1858, *CW* 3:106

28. Lincoln, First Debate at Ottawa, Illinois, Aug. 21, 1858, *CW* 3:16.

29. *CW* 3:16.

30. Lincoln, Speech in Columbus, Ohio, Sept. 16, 1859, *CW* 3:425.

31. Lincoln, Speech at Bloomington, Illinois, Sept. 4, 1858, *CW* 3:90.

32. Lincoln to Joshua Speed, Aug. 24, 1855, *CW* 2:320; First Debate with Stephen Douglas, Ottawa, Illinois, Aug, 21, 1858, *CW* 3:16.

33. Lincoln, Speech in Peoria, Illinois, Oct. 16, 1854, *CW* 2:274.

34. Lincoln, Speech Carlinville, Illinois, Aug. 31, 1858, *CW* 3:79.

35. Lincoln to James N. Brown, Oct. 18, 1858, *CW* 3:327–28.

4. Becoming President and Defending the Union

1. *New York Times*, Mar. 5, 1861.

2. Seward quote in Stephen Oates, *With Malice toward None: A Life of Abraham Lincoln* (New York: Harper, 1994), 221

3. Henry C. Whitney to William H. Herndon, Aug. 29, 1867, *HI* 636; on

Lincoln's reading habits, see Robert Bray, "What Lincoln Read—An Evaluative and Annotated List," *Journal of the Abraham Lincoln Association* 28 (Summer 2007), 28–81.

4. "Spot" Resolutions, US House of Representatives, Dec. 22, 1847, *CW* 1:420–22; Speech on the War with Mexico, Jan. 12, 1848, *CW* 431–42; for good recent studies of Lincoln's opposition to the Mexican War, see Gabor S. Boritt, "Lincoln's Opposition to the Mexican War," and Mark E. Neely Jr., "War and Partisanship," in *Civil War History* 24 (Mar. 1978), 5–24.

5. US Constitution, Article I and Article IV.

6. US Constitution, Article II, Section 8.

7. *Bas v. Tingy* 4 US (4 Dall.) 37 (1800); *Martin v. Mott* 25 US (12 Wheat.) 19 (1827); *Dynes v. Hoover* 61 US (20 How.) 65 (1858); and Brian R. Dirck, *Waging War on Trial: A Handbook with Cases, Laws, and Documents* (Santa Barbara: ABC-CLIO, 2003), esp. 27–80.

8. See Alexander Hamilton, *Federalist* no. 84, Clinton Rossiter, ed., *The Federalist Papers* (New York: Signet, 2000), 480; on the general history of the writ, see William F. Duker, *A Constitutional History of Habeas Corpus* (Westport: Greenwood Press, 1980).

9. US Constitution, Article I, Section 9.

10. Jefferson Davis, Inaugural Address, Feb. 18, 1861, in Lynda Crist, et al., eds., *The Papers of Jefferson Davis* (Baton Rouge: Louisiana State University Press, 1971–2003), 7:45–51.

11. See generally Elbert B. Smith, *The Presidency of James Buchanan* (Lawrence: University Press of Kansas, 1975), chaps. 12–14; and Kenneth M. Stampp's succinct but useful assessment of Buchanan in America in *1857: A Nation on the Brink* (New York: Oxford University Press, 1990), 46–50.

12. *New York World*, quoted in Kenneth M. Stampp, *And the War Came: The North and the Secession Crisis, 1860–1861* (Baton Rouge: Louisiana State University Press, 1950), 61.

13. Lincoln to Elihu Washburn, Dec. 21, 1860, *CW* 4:159.

14. Text of Buchanan's speech at <http://teachingamericanhistory.org/library/index.asp?document=946>, accessed July 8, 2010; my analysis of Buchanan's constitutional thought has been influenced by Elbert G. Smith's excellent and balanced *The Presidency of James Buchanan* (Lawrence: University Press of Kansas, 1975); and Jean Baker's more recent *James Buchanan* (New York: Times Books, 2004), esp. 4–5, 22, 77, and passim, which roots his constitutional thought in a rigid intellectual worldview.

15. Hale quote in *Congressional Globe*, 36th Congress, 2nd session, 9–10.

16. Smith, *Presidency of James Buchanan*, 186–87.

17. Text of the resolutions at <http://avalon.law.yale.edu/19th_century/critten.asp>, accessed July 11, 2010; see also David Kyvig, *Explicit and Authentic Acts: Amending the US Constitution, 1776–1995* (Lawrence: University Press of Kansas, 1996), 146–50.

18. Potter, *Impending Crisis*, 530–32, offers a convincing analysis of the Crittenden Resolutions' proslavery tilt; Kyvig, *Explicit and Authentic Acts*, 150–52, offers a more sympathetic perspective on these matters.

19. Lincoln, Speech in Pittsburgh, Pennsylvania, Feb. 14, 1861, *CW* 4:209.

20. Lincoln, Speech at Philadelphia, Pennsylvania, Feb. 22, 1861, *CW* 4:240.

21. Davis, *Rise and Fall*, 1:98.

22. The best discussion of this remains Edwin S. Corwin's classic, *The "Higher Law" Background of American Constitutional Law* (Ithaca: Cornell University Press, 1955).

23. Samuel T. Spear, *The Law-Abiding Conscience, and the Higher Law Conscience: A Sermon* (New York: Lambert and Lane, 1850), 25; see also William Hosmer, *The Higher Law, in its Relations to Civil Government, with Particular reference to Slavery, and the Fugitive Slave Law* (Auburn: Derby and Miller, 1857).

24. Text of Seward's speech at <http://eweb.furman.edu/~benson/docs/seward.htm>, accessed July 20, 2010.

25. Lincoln in fact made it a point to distance himself from Seward's speech; see Lincoln, Speech to the Springfield Scott Club, Aug. 14 and 26, 1852, *CW* 2:156; and Foner, *The Fiery Trial*, 86–87.

5. The War, Civil Liberties, and *Ex Parte Merryman*

1. Swisher, *Roger Taney*, 536–37, 567; Taney quotes in James F. Simon, *Lincoln and Chief Justice Taney: Slavery, Secession, and the President's War Powers* (New York: Simon and Schuster, 2006), 194, 337fn.; on Taney's views concerning secession, see Don E. Fehrenbacher, "Roger B. Taney and the Sectional Crisis," *Journal of Southern History* 43 (Nov. 1977), 558.

2. Samuel Tyler, *Memoir of Roger Brooke Taney, LLD.: Chief Justice of the Supreme Court of the United States* (Baltimore: John Murphy, 1872), 458; on Taney's general disdain for Lincoln, see Robert M. Spector, "Lincoln and Taney: A Study in Constitutional Polarization," *American Journal of Legal History* 15 (July 1971), 204–5.

3. US Constitution, Article II, Section 3; Lincoln, Proclamation Calling Militia and Convening Congress, Apr. 15, 1861, *CW* 4:332.

4. Mason letter reprinted in Frank Moore, ed., *The Rebellion Record: A Diary of American Events, with Documents* (New York: G. P. Putnam, 1861), 254.

5. Lincoln to Orville H. Browning, Sept. 22, 1861, *CW* 4:532.

6. See generally Otis K. Rice and Stephen W. Brown, *West Virginia: A History* (Lexington: University Press of Kentucky, 1985), 114–18.

7. Ibid., 118–21; Lincoln to Simon Cameron, Sept. 6, 1861, *CW* 4:511.

8. Rice and Brown, *West Virginia: A History*, 122.

9. US. Constitution, Article IV, Section 3.

10. Lincoln to Members of Cabinet, Dec. 23, 1862, *CW* 6:18.

11. Lincoln, Opinion on the Admission of West Virginia into the Union, Dec. 31, 1862, *CW* 6:26–28.

12. Burlingame, *Inside Lincoln's White House*, 18; see also entry concerning Maryland legislature, 12; on Annapolis, see *Scientific American* 4 (New York: Munn and Co., 1861), 290; Montgomery Meigs to Abraham Lincoln, May 10, 1861, Abraham Lincoln Papers, Library of Congress (hereinafter referred to as LPLC); and Oliver Dyer to Abraham Lincoln, May 2, 1861, LPLC; Thomas Hicks to Abraham Lincoln, May 8, 1861, LPLC.

13. Salmon P. Chase to Abraham Lincoln, Apr. 25, 1861, LPLC; John P. Kennedy, "An Appeal to Maryland," *Rebellion Record* 1:374.

14. Salmon P. Chase to Abraham Lincoln, Apr. 25, 1861, LPLC.

15. US Constitution, Article I, Section 9; on the opinions of legal authorities such as Joseph Story on this matter, see Mark E. Neely's excellent discussion in *The Fate of Liberty: Abraham Lincoln and Civil Liberties* (Cambridge: Oxford University Press, 1991), 4–5.

16. George William Brown, *Baltimore and the Nineteenth of April, 1861: A Study of the War* (Baltimore: N. Murray, 1887), 85–86.

17. John M. Hay and John G. Nicolay, *Abraham Lincoln: A History* (New York: Century, 1890), 153.

18. Lincoln to Winfield Scott, Apr. 27, 1861, *CW* 4:347; Neely, *Fate of Liberty*, 9.

19. Neely, *Fate of Liberty*, 8–9.

20. Mitchell, *Maryland Voices*, 94.

21. Proclamation Suspending the Writ of Habeas Corpus in Florida, May 10, 1861, *CW* 4:364–65; Neely, *Fate of Liberty*, 9–10.

22. Lincoln to Winfield Scott, July 2, 1861, *CW* 4:419.

23. Neely, *Fate of Liberty*, 10.

24. Sir William Howard Russell, *Mr. Russell on Bull Run with a Note; from the Rebellion Record* (New York: G. P. Putnam, 1861), 34.

25. Speech of M. S. Latham of California, US Senate, July 20, 1861, *Congressional Globe*, 37th Congress, 1st session, (Washington, DC: Congressional Globe Office, 1861), 19; Tatlow Jackson, "Authorities Cited Antagonistic to Horace Binney's Conclusions on the Writ of Habeas Corpus," in David Boyer Brown, *Decision of Chief Justice Taney in the Merryman Case, upon the Writ of Habeas Corpus* (Philadelphia: John Campbell, 1862), 43.

26. For the specifics on Merryman's background and case, see Sherrill Halbert, "The Suspension of the Writ of Habeas Corpus by President Lincoln," *American Journal of Legal History* 2 (Apr. 1958), 99–100.

27. Mark E. Neely Jr., "The Constitution and Civil Liberties under Lincoln," in Eric Foner, ed., *Our Lincoln: New Perspectives on Lincoln and His World* (New York: W. W. Norton, 2008), 36–42.

28. The text of the Merryman case itself contains a description of Merryman's arrest; see <http://teachingamericanhistory.org/library/index. asp?document=442>, accessed Aug. 9, 2010; for other information on Merryman's arrest, see Neely, "Constitution and Civil Liberties under Lincoln," 36; and James F. Simon's detailed description in *Lincoln and Chief Justice Taney: Slavery, Secession, and the President's War Powers* (New York: Simon and Schuster, 2006), 186–87.

29. http://teachingamericanhistory.org/library/index.asp?document=442>, accessed Aug. 9, 2010.

30. Ibid.

31. On Taney's lifelong dislike of excessive presidential power, see Spector, "Lincoln and Taney," 205–6.

32. http://teachingamericanhistory.org/library/index.asp?document=442>, accessed Aug. 9, 2010.

33. For a more sympathetic reading of Merryman, see Farber, *Lincoln's Constitution*, 158–59.

34. http://teachingamericanhistory.org/library/index.asp?document=442>, accessed Aug. 9, 2010.

35. On the public reaction to the Merryman controversy, see Simon, *Lincoln and Taney*, 188–90; Taney quote on 189.

36. Lincoln, Message to Congress in Special Session, July 4, 1861, *CW* 4:430.

37. Reverdy Johnson to Abraham Lincoln, June 17, 1861, LPLC; and William Seward to Abraham Lincoln, Apr. 1861, LPLC; Bates's opinion supporting the administration's policies is in Bates to Abraham Lincoln, July 5, 1861, LPLC.

38. See Mark Neely's analysis of this affair in *Fate of Liberty*, 17–18.

39. Neely, *Fate of Liberty*, 219–35 and passim.

40. On the aftermath of the Merryman arrest, see Simon, *Lincoln and Chief Justice Taney*, 197–98.

6. Congress and Winning the War

1. Burlingame, *Lincoln Observed*, 22.

2. Charles Sumner, *An Oration Delivered by Hon. Charles Sumner under the Auspices of the Young Men's Republican Union of New York* (New York: Young Men's Republican Union, 1861), 11; Wade quote in Hans L. Trefousse, *The Radical Republicans: Lincoln's Vanguard for Racial*

Justice (Baton Rouge: Louisiana State University Press, 1968), 171.

3. On Republicans and the Homestead Act, see Heather Cox Richardson, *The Greatest Nation of the Earth: Republican Economic Policies during the Civil War* (Cambridge: Harvard University Press, 1997), 144–50.

4. See Richardson, chaps. 4–6 and passim; text of Morrill Act at <http://ourdocuments.gov/doc.php?flash=true&doc=33&page=transcript>, accessed May 28, 2011.

5. George B. McClellan to Mary Ellen McClellan, July 27, 1861, in Stephen W. Sears, ed., *The Civil War Papers of George B. McClellan: Selected Correspondence, 1860–1865* (New York: DaCapo Press, 1992), 70; *New York Times*, July 20, 1861.

6. On McClellan's political ambitions, see Sears, *Little Napoleon*, 118, 154–56.

7. Hay, *Inside Lincoln's White House*, 27.

8. Historian Michael Les Benedict is the best authority on the various divisions and issues within Radical Republican ranks; see his seminal "Preserving the Constitution: The Conservative Basis of Radical Reconstruction," *Journal of American History* 61 (June 1974), 65–90; and his *A Compromise of Principle: Congressional Republicans and Reconstruction* (New York: W. W. Norton, 1974).

9. See generally *Index to the Congressional Globe, First Session, Thirty-Seventh Congress* (Washington, DC: Government Printing Office, 1863); also useful is David P. Currie, "The Civil War Congress," *University of Chicago Law Review* 73 (Autumn 2006), 1131–40.

10. Stevens quoted in Fawn M. Brodie, *Thaddeus Stevens: Scourge of the South* (New York: W. W. Norton, 1959), 164.

11. See on this point the speech of James W. Grimes, *Congressional Globe*, 37th Cong., 1st sess., 30.

12. Speech of William P. Fessenden, *Grimes*, 30–31.

13. A good recent overview of Lincoln's problems with Cameron can be found in Doris Kearns Goodwin's immensely popular (and thoroughly detailed) account of Lincoln's relationship with his cabinet members in *Team of Rivals: The Political Genius of Abraham Lincoln* (New York: Simon and Schuster, 2005), 410–17.

14. On Lincoln's administration as commander in chief, see James M. McPherson, *Tried by War: Abraham Lincoln as Commander in Chief* (New York: Penguin Press, 2008).

15. On the informal interview in Jan., see Arthur Tappan Pierson, *Zachariah Chandler; an Outline Sketch of His Life and Public Services* (Detroit: Post and Tribune, 1880), 224.

16. For a convincing assessment of the committee's military shortcomings, see Bruce Tap's definitive study of the committee, *Over Lincoln's Shoulder: The Committee on the Conduct of the War* (Lawrence: University Press of Kansas, 1998), 38–50, and passim.

17. Pierson, *Zachariah Chandler*, 225–26.

18. George B. McClellan to Abraham Lincoln, Jan. 15, 1862, LPLC.

19. Tap, *Over Lincoln's Shoulder*, 8.

20. Tap, *Over Lincoln's Shoulder*, 193–96.

21. Tap, *Over Lincoln's Shoulder*, 112–13.

22. On these meetings between members of the Committee and Lincoln, see Benjamin F. Wade to Abraham Lincoln, Dec. 31, 1861; Apr. 2, 1862; and Feb. 14, 1862, LPLC; on Lincoln's cooperative attitude towards congressional committees, see Harold M. Hyman, "Lincoln and Congress: Why Congress and Not Lincoln?" in Thomas F. Schwartz, ed., *For a Vast Future Also: Essays from the Journal of the Abraham Lincoln Association* (New York: Fordham University Press, 1999), 192–99.

23. Thomas A. Scott to Abraham Lincoln, Dec. 28, 1861, LPLC; Tap, *Over Lincoln's Shoulder*, 113.

24. Hay at this point was serving as a major in the army; see "News from Washington," *New York Times*, Mar. 25, 1864; and Burlingame, *Inside Lincoln's White House*, 183.

7. Lincoln and the Radicals

1. Lincoln, Appeal to Border State Representatives, July 12, 1862, *CW* 5:318; Susie King quote in James M. McPherson, *Marching toward Freedom: The Negro in the Civil War* (New York: Alfred A. Knopf, 1967), 35.

2. McPherson, *Marching toward Freedom*, 210; Hondon B. Hargrove, *Black Union Soldiers in the Civil War* (Jefferson, NC: McFarland, 1988), 13.

3. <http://mac110.assumption.edu/aas/Reports/confiscation1.html>, accessed Nov. 7, 2010.

4. US Constitution, Article III, Section 3.

5. Lincoln, Message to the Senate and the House of Representatives, July 17, 1862, *CW* 5:331.

6. Burlingame, *Lincoln: A Life*, 2:357–359, has a good discussion of these issues.

7. John C. Fremont, Proclamation, Aug. 30, 1861, United States War Department, *War of the Rebellion: A Compilation of the Official Records of the Union and Confederate Armies* (Washington, DC: Government Printing Office, 1880-1901).

8. Rpt. in *New York Times*, Sept. 1, 1861; and Frank Moore and Edward Everett, eds., *The Rebellion Record: A Diary of American Events* (New York: G. P. Putnam, 1861), 3:37.

9. Lincoln to John C. Fremont, Sept. 2, 1861, *CW* 4:506.

10. Burlingame, *Inside Lincoln's White House*, 123; for a good description of these events, see Burlingame, *Lincoln: A Life*, 2:202–4.

11. Lincoln to Orville Browning, Sept. 22, 1861, *CW* 4:531–32.

12. Wade quoted in Allen C. Guelzo, *Lincoln's Emancipation Proclamation: The End of Slavery in America* (New York: Simon and Schuster, 2006), 57; Resolutions Adopted by a Meeting of German Citizens, Chicago, Illinois, Nov. 9, 1861, in Moore, *Rebellion Record*, 3:344; also Foner, *The Fiery Trial*, 209.

13. General Orders no. 11, Department of the South, May 9, 1862, *OR*, Ser. I, 14:341.

14. Lincoln, Proclamation Revoking General Hunter's Order of Military Emancipation, May 9, 1862, *CW* 5:222.

15. Lincoln to Salmon P. Chase, May 17, 1862, *CW* 5:219.

16. Quoted in Chandra Manning, *What This Cruel War Was Over: Soldiers, Slavery, and the Civil War* (New York: Vintage Books, 2007), 75.

17. Greeley, "Prayer of Twenty Millions," *New York Tribune*, Aug. 19, 1862.

18. Lincoln, reply to Horace Greeley, Aug. 22, 1862, *CW* 5:388.

19. Lincoln to John A. Gilmer, Dec. 1860, *CW* 4:152.

20. Lincoln to Albert G. Hodges. Apr. 4, 1864, *CW* 7:281–82.

21. Francis B. Carpenter, *The Inner Life of Abraham Lincoln: Six Months at the White House* (Lincoln: University of Nebraska Press, 1995; originally published in 1880), 21.

22. Lincoln to Albert G. Hodges. Apr. 4, 1864, *CW* 7:281–82.

23. Preliminary Confiscation Act, Sept. 22, 1862, *CW* 5:433–36.

24. Lincoln, Annual Message to Congress, Dec. 1, 1862, *CW* 5:530–34; Kyvig, *Explicit and Authentic Acts*, 129–31; amendment proposals in this period usually originated from Congress or state legislatures.

25. Lincoln, Annual Message to Congress, Dec. 1, 1862, *CW* 5:537.

26. Lincoln, Address on Colonization to a Deputation of Negroes, Aug. 14, 1862, *CW* 5:370–75.

27. Lincoln, Annual Message to Congress, Dec. 1, 1862, *CW* 5:537.

28. Emancipation Proclamation, Jan. 1, 1863, *CW* 6 29.

29. Lincoln to John A. McClernand, Jan. 8, 1863, *CW* 6:48; interview with Alexander W. Randall and Joseph T. Mills, Aug. 19, 1864, *CW* 7:507.

30. On this point, see Lincoln to Stephen A. Hurlbut, July 31, 1863, *CW* 6:358.

31. On this point, see Foner's recent and convincing assessment of Lincoln, compensation, and colonization in *The Fiery Trial*, 244–45, 252, 283, and passim.

8. The War and African Americans

1. Belz, *American Constitution*, 1:175–77.

2. See e.g. the occasional references to "treason" in his Message to Congress in Special Session, July 4, 1861, *CW* 4:428, 432; Annual Message to Congress, Dec. 3, 1861, *CW* 5:47; Opinion on the Admission of West Virginia into the Union, Dec. 31, 1862, *CW* 6:27; note also Lincoln

to Erastus Corning and Others, June 12, 1863, *CW* 6:262, in which he specifically avoids the "treason" outlined in the Constitution as a foundation for military arrests.

3. Hyman and Weicek, *Equal Justice under Law*, 241.

4. Hyman and Weicek, *Equal Justice under Law*, 334; Belz, *American Constitution*, 1:303–4.

5. Hyman and Weicek, *Equal Justice under Law*, 141.

6. Opinion of Attorney General Bates on Citizenship, Nov. 29, 1862, text at <http://quod.lib.umich.edu/cgi/t/text/text-idx?c=moa;cc=moa;rgn=main;view=text;idno=AEW6575.0001.001>, accessed Nov. 28, 2010.

7. Beverly Wilson Palmer, ed., *The Selected Letters of Charles Sumner* (Boston: Northeastern University Press, 1990), 1:253; *Foner, Fiery Trial*, 295.

8. Burlingame, *At Lincoln's Side*, 101.

9. Burlingame, *At Lincoln's Side*, 69.

10. Lincoln, Proclamation of Amnesty and Reconstruction, Dec. 8, 1863, *CW* 7:53–56.

11. Text of the Second Confiscation Act at <http://www.history.umd.edu/Freedmen/conact2.htm>, accessed Nov. 30, 2010; Lincoln, Annual Address to Congress, Dec. 8, 1863, *CW* 7:50.

12. Lincoln, Proclamation of Amnesty and Reconstruction, Dec. 8, 1863, *CW* 7:55.

13. Text of Wade-Davis Bill at <http://www.civilwar.org/education/history/primarysources/wade-davis-bill.html>, accessed Dec. 1, 2010.

14. Lincoln, Proclamation Concerning Reconstruction, July 8, 1864, *CW* 7:433–34.

15. Burlingame, *Inside Lincoln's White House*, 217.

16. Burlingame, *Inside Lincoln's White House*, 217–18.

17. Burlingame, *Inside Lincoln's White House*, 218.

18. Burlingame, *Inside Lincoln's White House*, 218–19.

19. "Protest of Senator Wade and H. Davis," in *The American Cyclopaedia and Register of Important Events of the Year 1864* (New York: D. Appleton, 1869), 4:307fn; Brooks, *Lincoln Observed*, 185.

20. See e.g. Lincoln, Speech in Tremont, Illinois, May 2, 1840, *CW* 1:210.

21. Lincoln to James S. Wadsworth, c. Jan. 1864, *CW* 7:101.

22. Lincoln to Michael Hahn, Mar. 13, 1864, *CW* 7:243.

23. See Foner's assessment of Lincoln and the suffrage issue in *The Fiery Trial*, 319.

24. See generally Michael S. Vorenberg, *Final Freedom: The Civil War, the Abolition of Slavery, and the Thirteenth Amendment* (Cambridge: Cambridge University Press, 2004); and Herman Belz, *Emancipation and Equal Rights: Politics and Constitutionalism in the Civil War Era* (New York: W. W. Norton, 1978), 110–14.

25. Burlingame, *Inside Lincoln's White House*, 218.

26. Foner, *The Fiery Trial*, 312; also Burlingame, *Lincoln: A Life*, 2:745–51.
27. Charles *Sumner, The Works of Charles Sumner* (Boston: Lee and Shepard, 1873), 8:78.
28. Lincoln, Response to Serenade, Feb. 1, 1865, *CW* 8:254.
29. Lincoln, Last Public Address, Apr. 11, 1865, *CW* 8:403.
30. Booth quote in Henry Clay Whitney, *Life of Lincoln: Lincoln, the President* (New York: Baker and Taylor, 1908), 2:322.

Epilogue

1. Lincoln to Zachariah Chandler, Nov. 20, 1863, *CW* 7:24.
2. Douglass, "Oration in Memory of Abraham Lincoln," Apr. 14, 1876; text at <http://teachingamericanhistory.org/library/index.asp?documentprint=39>, accessed Dec. 4, 2010.

BIBLIOGRAPHY

Abbott, John S. C. *South and North; or, Impressions Received during a Trip to Cuba and the South.* New York: Abbey and Abbott, 1860.

Abraham Lincoln Papers, Library of Congress.

Adams, John Quincy. *Memoirs of John Quincy Adams.* Philadelphia: J. P. Lippincott, 1877.

Anastoplo, George. *Abraham Lincoln: A Constitutional Biography.* New York: Rowman and Littlefield, 2001.

Basler, Roy P., ed. *Collected Works of Abraham Lincoln.* 9 vols. New Brunswick: Rutgers University Press, 1953.

Belz, Herman. *Emancipation and Equal Rights: Politics and Constitutionalism in the Civil War Era.* New York: W. W. Norton, 1978.

Benedict, Michael Les. *A Compromise of Principle: Congressional Republicans and Reconstruction.* New York: W. W. Norton, 1974.

———. *The Fruits of Victory: Alternatives in Restoring the Union, 1865–1877,* rev. ed. Lanham, MD: Library of America, 1986.

———. "Preserving the Constitution: The Conservative Basis of Radical Reconstruction." *Journal of American History* 61 (June 1974): 65–90.

Bilotta, James D. *Race and the Rise of the Republican Party, 1848–1865.* New York: Peter Lang, 1992.

Blackstone, Sir William. *Commentaries on the Laws of England, in Four Books,* 13th ed. London: A Strahan, 1800.

Boritt, Gabor S. *Lincoln and the Economics of the American Dream,* 2nd ed. Urbana: University of Illinois Press, 1992.

Bray, Robert. *Reading with Lincoln.* Carbondale: Southern Illinois University Press, 2010.

Brodie, Fawn M. *Thaddeus Stevens: Scourge of the South.* New York: W. W. Norton, 1959.

Brookhiser, Richard. *Founding Father: Rediscovering George Washington.* New York: Free Press, 1997.

Brown, David Boyer. *Decision of Chief Justice Taney in the Merryman Case, upon the Writ of Habeas Corpus.* Philadelphia: John Campbell, 1862.

Brown, George William. *Baltimore and the Nineteenth of April, 1861: A Study of the War.* Baltimore: N. Murray, 1887.

Burlingame, Michael. *At Lincoln's Side: John Hay's Civil War Correspondence and Selected Writings.* Carbondale: Southern Illinois University Press, 2000.

———. *The Inner World of Abraham Lincoln.* Urbana: University of Illinois Press, 1997.

———. *Lincoln: A Life.* 2 vols. Baltimore: Johns Hopkins University Press, 2008.

———. *Lincoln Observed: The Civil War Dispatches of Noah Brooks.* Baltimore: Johns Hopkins University Press, 2002.

Burlingame, Michael, and John R. Ettlinger, eds. *Inside Lincoln's White House: The Complete Civil War Diary of John Hay.* Carbondale: Southern Illinois University Press, 1999.

Carpenter, Francis B. *The Inner Life of Abraham Lincoln: Six Months at the White House.* 1880. Rpt. Lincoln: University of Nebraska Press, 1995.

Cluskey, Michael W., ed. *The Political Textbook, or Encyclopedia, Containing Everything Necessary for the Reference of the Politicians and Statesmen of the United States,* 2nd ed. Philadelphia: James B. Smith, 1858.

Corwin, Edwin S. *The "Higher Law" Background of American Constitutional Law.* Ithaca: Cornell University Press, 1955.

Crist, Lynda, et al., eds. *The Papers of Jefferson Davis.* 11 vols. Baton Rouge: Louisiana State University Press, 1971–2003.

Currie, David P. "The Civil War Congress." *University of Chicago Law Review* 73 (Autumn 2006): 1131–226.

Davis, Jefferson. *The Rise and Fall of the Confederate Government.* 1881. 2 vols. Rpt. New York: DaCapo, 1992.

Dirck, Brian, ed. *Lincoln Emancipated: The President and the Politics of Race.* Carbondale: Southern Illinois University Press, 2007.

———. *Waging War on Trial: A Handbook with Cases, Laws, and Documents.* Santa Barbara: ABC-CLIO, 2003.

Donald, David H. *Lincoln.* New York: Simon and Schuster, 1995.

Duker, William F. *A Constitutional History of Habeas Corpus.* Westport: Greenwood, 1980.

Edge, Frederick Milnes. *Slavery Doomed; or, the Contest between Free and Slave Labor in the United States.* London: Smith, Elder, 1860.

Ellet, Charles. *The Army of the Potomac, and Its Mismanagement; Respectfully Addressed to Congress.* New York: Ross and Tousey, 1862.

Executive Committee of the American Anti-slavery Society. *Slavery and the Internal Slave Trade in the United States of North America.* London: Thomas Ward, 1841.

Moore, Frank, and Edward Everett, eds., *The Rebellion Record: A Diary of American Events* (New York: G. P. Putnam, 1861).

Farber, Daniel. *Lincoln's Constitution.* Chicago: University of Chicago Press, 2003.

Fehrenbacher, Donald E. *The Dred Scott Case: Its Significance in Law and Politics.* New York: Oxford University Press, 1978.

———. "Roger B. Taney and the Sectional Crisis." *Journal of Southern History* 43 (Nov. 1977): 558–74.

Fehrenbacher, Donald E., and Virginia Fehrenbacher, eds. *Recollected Words of Abraham Lincoln.* Stanford: Stanford University Press, 1996.

Fletcher, George P. *Our Secret Constitution: How Lincoln Redefined American Democracy*. Cambridge: Oxford University Press, 2001.

Foner, Eric. *The Fiery Trial: Abraham Lincoln and American Slavery*. New York: W. W. Norton, 2010.

———. *Free Soil, Free Labor, Free Men: The Ideology of the Republican Party before the Civil War*, 2nd ed. Oxford: Oxford University Press, 1995.

———, ed. *Our Lincoln: New Perspectives On Lincoln and His World*. New York: W. W. Norton, 2008.

Forbes, Robert Pierce. *The Missouri Compromise and Its Aftermath: Slavery and the Meaning of America*. Chapel Hill: University of North Carolina Press, 2007.

Fornieri, Joseph R., and Sara Vaughn Gabbard, eds. *Lincoln's America, 1809–1865*. Carbondale: Southern Illinois University Press, 2008.

Fredrickson, George M. *Big Enough to Be Inconsistent: Abraham Lincoln Confronts Slavery and Race*. Cambridge: Harvard University Press, 2008.

Gales, Joseph, et al., eds. *Register of the Debates in Congress, Compromising the Leading Debates and Incidents of the Twentieth Congress*. Washington, DC: Gales and Eaton, 1828.

Goodwin, Doris Kearns. *Team of Rivals: The Political Genius of Abraham Lincoln*. New York: Simon and Schuster, 2005.

Guelzo, Allen C. *Lincoln's Emancipation Proclamation: The End of Slavery in America*. New York: Simon and Schuster, 2006.

Halbert, Sherrill. "The Suspension of the Writ of Habeas Corpus by President Lincoln." *American Journal of Legal History* 2 (Apr. 1958): 95–116.

Hamilton, Holman. *Prologue to Conflict: The Crisis and Compromise of 1850*, 2nd ed. Lexington: University of Kentucky Press, 2005.

Hargrove, Hondon B. *Black Union Soldiers in the Civil War*. Jefferson, NC: McFarland, 1988.

Harrold, Stanley. *Subversives: Antislavery Community in Washington, DC, 1828–1865*. Baton Rouge: Louisiana State University Press, 2003.

Hartog, Hendrik. "The Constitution of Aspiration and 'The Rights That Belong to Us All.'" *Journal of American History* 74 (Dec. 1987): 1013–34.

Hay, John M., and John G. Nicolay. *Abraham Lincoln: A History*. New York: Century, 1890.

Herndon, William H., and Jesse W. Weik. *Herndon's Lincoln*. 1889 and 1892. Rpt. Urbana: University of Illinois Press, 2006.

Holt, Michael F. *The Political Crises of the 1850s*. New York: W. W. Norton, 1983.

Hosmer, William. *The Higher Law, in Its Relations to Civil Government, with Particular Reference to Slavery, and the Fugitive Slave Law*. Auburn: Derby and Miller, 1857.

Huebner, Timothy S. *The Taney Court: Justices, Rulings, and Legacy*. Santa Barbara: ABC-CLIO, 2003.

Hyman, Harold M., and William M. Wiecek. *Equal Justice under Law: Constitutional Development, 1835–1875.* New York: Harper Torchbooks, 1982.

Johnson, Allen. *Stephen Douglas: A Study in American Politics.* New York: MacMillan, 1908.

Kauffman, Michael W. *American Brutus: John Wilkes Booth and the Lincoln Conspiracies.* New York: Random House, 2004.

Kettner, James H. *The Development of American Citizenship, 1608–1870.* Chapel Hill: University of North Carolina Press, 1978.

Kramer, Larry D. *The People Themselves: Popular Constitutionalism and Judicial Review.* Cambridge: Oxford University Press, 2005.

Kyvig, David. *Explicit and Authentic Acts: Amending the US Constitution, 1776–1995.* Lawrence: University Press of Kansas, 1996.

McPherson, Edward. *The Political History of the United States during the Great Rebellion.* Washington, DC: Philp and Solomons, 1864.

McPherson, James M. *Abraham Lincoln and the Second American Revolution.* Cambridge: Oxford University Press, 1992.

———. *Marching toward Freedom: The Negro in the Civil War.* New York: Alfred A. Knopf, 1967.

———, ed. *Our Lincoln: New Perspectives on Lincoln and His World.* New York: W. W. Norton, 2009.

———. *Tried by War: Abraham Lincoln as Commander in Chief.* New York: Penguin, 2008.

———, ed. *"We Cannot Escape History": Lincoln and Last Best Hope of Earth.* Urbana: University of Illinois Press, 1995.

Manning, Chandra. *What This Cruel War Was Over: Soldiers, Slavery, and the Civil War.* New York: Vintage, 2007.

Marshall, James V. *The United States Manual of Biography and History.* Philadelphia: James B. Smith, 1856.

Maury, Sara Mytton. *The Statesmen of America in 1846.* Philadelphia: Carey and Hart, 1846.

Mayer, David N. *The Constitutional Thought of Thomas Jefferson.* Charlottesville: University of Virginia Press, 1995.

Mendelberg, Tali. *The Race Card: Campaign Strategy: Implicit Messages, and the Norm of Equality.* Princeton: Princeton University Press, 2001.

Miller, Marion Millds, ed. *Life and Works of Abraham Lincoln.* 9 vols. New York: Current Literature, 1907.

Moore, Frank, ed. *The Rebellion Record: A Diary of American Events, with Documents.* New York: G. P. Putnam, 1861.

Moore, Glover. *The Missouri Controversy, 1819–1821.* Lexington: University of Kentucky Press, 1953.

Neely, Mark E., Jr. *The Fate of Liberty: Abraham Lincoln and Civil Liberties.* Cambridge: Oxford University Press, 1991.

———. *The Last Best Hope of Earth: Abraham Lincoln and the Promise of America*. Cambridge: Harvard University Press, 1995.

Newmyer, R. Kent. *The Supreme Court under Marshall and Taney*, 2nd ed. New York: Harlan Davidson, 2006.

Oates, Stephen B. *With Malice toward None: A Life of Abraham Lincoln*. New York: Harper, 1994.

Palmer, Beverly Wilson, ed. *The Selected Letters of Charles Sumner*. 2 vols. Boston: Northeastern University Press, 1990.

Paludan, Phillip S. *The Presidency of Abraham Lincoln*. Lawrence: University Press of Kansas, 1994.

Pierce, Edward Lillie, and Charles Sumner. *Memoir and Letters of Charles Sumner*. 4 vols. Boston: Roberts Bros., 1893.

Pierson, Arthur Tappan. *Zachariah Chandler; an Outline Sketch of His Life and Public Services*. Detroit: Post and Tribune, 1880.

Potter, David S. *The Impending Crisis, 1848–1860*. New York: Harper and Row, 1977.

Remini, Robert V. *Andrew Jackson and the Bank War*, 2nd ed. New York: W. W. Norton, 1967.

Richardson, Heather Cox. *The Greatest Nation of the Earth: Republican Economic Policies during the Civil War*. Cambridge: Harvard University Press, 1997.

———. *Henry Clay: Statesman for the Union*. New York: W. W. Norton, 1991.

Rice, Otis K., and Stephen W. Brown, *West Virginia: A History* (Lexington: University Press of Kentucky, 1985).

Rossiter, Clinton, ed., *The Federalist Papers* (New York: Signet, 2000).

Russell, Sir William Howard. *Mr. Russell on Bull Run with a Note; from the Rebellion Record*. New York: G. P. Putnam, 1861.

Schwartz, Thomas F, ed. *For a Vast Future Also: Essays from the Journal of the Abraham Lincoln Association*. New York: Fordham University Press, 1999.

Sears, Stephen W., ed. *The Civil War Papers of George B. McClellan: Selected Correspondence, 1860–1865*. New York: DaCapo, 1992.

———. *George B. McClellan: The Young Napoleon*. New York: DaCapo, 1999.

Sheahan, James Washington. *The Life of Stephen A. Douglas*. New York: Harper and Brothers, 1860.

Simon, James F. *Lincoln and Chief Justice Taney: Slavery, Secession, and the President's War Powers*. New York: Simon and Schuster, 2006.

Smith, Elbert B. *The Presidency of James Buchanan*. Lawrence: University Press of Kansas, 1975.

Spear, Samuel T. *The Law-abiding Conscience, and the Higher Law Conscience: A Sermon*. New York: Lambert and Lane, 1850.

Spector, Robert M. "Lincoln and Taney: A Study in Constitutional Polarization." *American Journal of Legal History* 15 (July 1971): 199–214.

Spooner, Lysander. *The Unconstitutionality of Slavery*. New York: Burt Franklin, 1860.

Stampp, Kenneth M. *America in 1857: A Nation on the Brink*. New York: Oxford University Press, 1990.

———. *And the War Came: The North and the Secession Crisis, 1860–1861*. Baton Rouge: Louisiana State University Press, 1950.

Stevens, Thaddeus. *Reconstruction: Speech of the Hon. Thaddeus Stevens, Delivered in the City of Lancaster, September 7, 1865*. Lancaster: Examiner and Herald, 1865.

Striner, Richard. *Father Abraham: Lincoln's Relentless Struggle to End Slavery*. Cambridge: Oxford University Press, 2007.

Sumner, Charles. *An Oration Delivered by Hon. Charles Sumner under the Auspices of the Young Men's Republican Union of New York*. New York: Young Men's Republican Union, 1861.

———. *Security and Reconciliation for the Future: Propositions and Arguments on the Reorganization of the Rebel States*. Boston: Rand and Avery, 1865.

Tap, Bruce. *Over Lincoln's Shoulder: The Committee on the Conduct of the War*. Lawrence: University Press of Kansas, 1998.

Thomas, Benjamin P. *Lincoln's New Salem*, 2nd ed. Carbondale: Southern Illinois University Press, 1988.

Trefousse, Hans L. *The Radical Republicans: Lincoln's Vanguard for Racial Justice*. Baton Rouge: Louisiana State University Press, 1968.

Tyler, Samuel, and Roger B. Taney. *Memoir of Roger Brooke Taney, LLD* Baltimore: John Murphy, 1872.

United States War Department, *War of the Rebellion: A Compilation of the Official Records of the Union and Confederate Armies* (Washington DC: Government Printing Office, 1880-1901).

Vorenberg, Michael S. *Final Freedom: The Civil War, the Abolition of Slavery, and the Thirteenth Amendment*. Cambridge: Cambridge University Press, 2004.

Washburn, Israel. *The Issues: The Dred Scott Decision: The Parties. Speech of Hon. Israel Washburn, Jun., of Maine, Delivered in the House of Representatives, May 19, 1860*. Washington, DC: Congressional Republican Committee, 1860.

Weems, Mason Locke. *Life of George Washington*. Philadelphia: Joseph Allen, 1833.

Wesley, John. *Views of American Slavery, Taken a Century Ago*. Philadelphia: Assoc. of Friends, 1858.

Whitney, Henry Clay. *Life of Lincoln: Lincoln, the President*. 2 vols. New York: Baker and Taylor, 1908.

Wiecek, William M. *The Sources of Antislavery Constitutionalism*. Ithaca: Cornell University Press, 1977.

Wilson, Douglas L., and Rodney O. Davis, eds. *Herndon's Informants: Letters, Interviews, and Statements about Abraham Lincoln*. Urbana: University of Illinois Press, 1997.

———. *Honor's Voice: The Transformation of Abraham Lincoln*. New York: Vintage, 1999.

Winkle, Kenneth J. *Young Eagle: The Rise of Abraham Lincoln*. New York: Taylor, 2001.

INDEX

abolitionism, 13, 15, 31, 33, 35, 45, 58, 64–66, 74

Adams, John Quincy, 20

African Americans: and Abraham Lincoln, 44–48; and citizenship, 118–23, 129; and colonization, 111–12; as contraband, 100–101; and *Dred Scott v. Sanford* (1857), 36–37; and emancipation, 111–12; as soldiers, 96, 97, 114, 125–28, 130; and Stephen Douglas, 45; suffrage, 1, 2, 125–26, 130, 131

Anastoplo, George, 2

Articles of Association (1774), 63

Articles of Confederation (1778), 63

Baker, Edward, 91

Ball's Bluff, Battle of, 90–91, 93, 94

Bates, Edward, 84, 119

Blackstone, Sir William, 8

blockade, 53, 117–18

Bloomington, Illinois, 25

Booth, John Wilkes, 1, 2, 130

border states, 69, 101, 103–5, 110–11, 113, 116

broad constructionism, 9–10, 20, 31, 61, 88, 108, 113, 132

Brooks, Noah, 125–26

Buchanan, James, 57–60, 67, 68, 72, 89

Bull Run, First Battle of, 92, 93, 97

Butler, Benjamin, 100–101, 108

cabinet, presidential, 54, 71, 86

Cadwalader, George, 79, 82

Cameron, Simon, 92–93, 97

Cass, Lewis, 22

Chandler, Zachariah, 86, 94–95, 124–25, 131

Chase, Salmon, 74

Civil Rights Act (1866), 132

Clay, Henry, 19, 21, 28, 110

colonization, 110–12

compensated emancipation, 110–11

Compromise of 1820, 19, 21, 22, 23, 38, 59

Compromise of 1850, 21

Confederate States of America: 56, 57, 63–64, 115–18

Confiscation Act, First (1861), 101, 108

Confiscation Act, Second (1862), 101–3, 108, 122

Congress (U.S.), 3, 10, 11, 38, 58: and Reconstruction, 120–26, 130–34; and slavery, 15, 17, 21, 24, 61–62, 100–109; and war-making powers, 53–56, 133; and Western territories, 38

Constitution (U.S.): amendments proposed, 59–60, 128–29; and citizenship, 118–22, 129; commerce clause, 108; and *Dred Scott v. Sanford* (1857), 35–49, 102, 119; and due process, 102; Fifteenth Amendment, 1, 2, 132; Fifth Amendment, 37–38, 102, 113; Fourteenth Amendment, 132; fugitive slave clause, 18, 36, 48, 61; general welfare clause, 10; guarantee clause, 121, 123–24, 133; and habeas corpus, 55–56, 74–85; necessary and proper clause, 10–11, 108; and new states, 70–72; and originalism, 29–30; pardoning power, 122–23, 125; preamble, 63; and presidency, 53–56, 69, 124–26, 128; and separation of powers, 53, 125, 128; and slave trade, 37; and slavery, 13, 35, 61, 128–30; and Southerners, 34–35, 61–62; Thirteenth Amendment, 1, 2, 128–30; three-fifths clause, 25; and treason, 102, 104, 115–16; unamendable amendment proposed, 59–60; and war, 52–56, 81–82, 91, 108, 113, 117, 120, 124; and Western territories, 18, 22, 24, 37–38, 42–43, 61, 108

Crittenden, John, 59–60

Crittenden Committee, 59–61

Curtis, Benjamin, 37

Davis, Henry Winter, 123
Davis, Jefferson, 21, 56, 63–64, 74, 116
Declaration of Independence, 7, 13, 27–32–37, 39–41, 44–52, 56, 60–61, 65–66, 107, 112, 134
Democratic Party, 9, 22, 28, 33–34, 42, 43, 89, 91, 93
Douglas, Stephen, 17, 20–22, 24, 31, 33–34, 42–50, 67, 134
Douglass, Frederick, 131
Dred Scott v. Sanford (1857), 35–49, 80, 102, 119, 123
Dyer, Oliver, 74

emancipation, 99, 103–14, 119–20
Emancipation Proclamation, 107–8, 110, 113–14, 119
England, 115
Ex Parte Merryman (1861), 78–84, 116
Ex Parte Milligan (1866), 133

Farber, Daniel, 2
Federalist Party, 9, 14
Fessenden, William Pitt, 92
Fillmore, Millard, 21
Fletcher, George P., 2
Florida, 76
Foner, Eric, 129
Fort McHenry, Maryland, 79
Fort Pulaski, Georgia, 100
Fort Sumter, South Carolina, 69
Founding Fathers, 4, 6, 9, 10, 11–13, 25, 27–29, 52–56, 75, 82, 102, 107, 116, 120, 128, 134
France, 115
Freedmen's Bureau, 132
Freeport doctrine, 42–44
Fremont, John C., 103–6

Garrison, William Lloyd, 28
Greely, Horace, 106–7

habeas corpus, writ of, 55–56, 74–85, 99
Habeas Corpus Act (1863), 84, 98
Hahn, Michael, 127, 130
Hale, John P., 58, 60

Hamilton, Alexander, 9, 10, 14, 31, 88, 113
Hamiltonian constitutionalism. *See* broad constructionism
Hartog, Hendrik, 4
Hay, John, 121, 125
Herndon, William, 23, 24
Herold, David, 1, 130
Hicks, Thomas, 74
higher law, 64–66, 72, 87
Homestead Act (1862), 88, 89
Hunter, David, 105

Illinois Senate race (1858), 42–50
Ingersoll, Charles, 23
iron clad oath, 123

Jackson, Andrew, 88
Jefferson, Thomas, 10, 14, 18, 27, 31, 88
Jeffersonian-Republican Party, 10
Johnson, Andrew, 132
Johnson, Reverdy, 84
Joint Committee on the Conduct of the War, 91–98
Judicial review, 40–41
Julian, George, 86

Kansas-Nebraska Act (1854), 17–18, 22–23, 27–29, 31, 33
Keitt, Laurence, 35
Kentucky, 69
Kentucky Resolution (1799), 14
King, Susie, 100

Lee, Robert E., 1, 130
Legal Tender Act (1862), 88
Lincoln, Abraham: and abolitionism, 16, 31, 33, 46; and African American suffrage, 1–2, 125–28, 130, 131; and broad constructionism, 10–12, 24, 108, 113; and civil liberties during Civil War, 83–85, 99; and civil religion, 7; and colonization 110–12; as commander-in-chief, 52–56, 91–93, 97, 105, 107–10, 113–14, 120, 121, 132; and compensated emancipation,

110–11; and Compromise of 1820, 19; and Compromise of 1850, 24; and confiscation acts, 101–3, 110; and Congress, 87–89, 91, 96–98, 110–13, 120–25, 128–30, 133; as congressman, 23, 52; conservatism of, 8, 52; criticism of, 86, 91; and Crittenden Committee, 61; and Declaration of Independence, 7, 27–32, 33, 39–51; 56; 60–61, 63, 65–66, 107, 112; and Stephen Douglas, 24–26; and *Dred Scott v. Sanford* (1857), 39–50; early exposure to Constitution, 6–8; and economic development, 10, 11, 12, 24, 87–89, 132; elasticity of constitutionalism, 72, 98, 99, 102–3; and emancipation, 99, 103–14, 124–25; and Emancipation Proclamation, 110–14; and *ex parte Merryman*, 83–85; and first inaugural address (1861), 60–63, 72; and Founding Fathers, 6–8, 11–12, 25–29; and Fremont's emancipation decree, 103–5; and fugitive slaves, 48; and habeas corpus, 74–85, 98, 99; and Hunter's emancipation decree, 105; and Illinois Senate race (1858), 33, 42–50; as Illinois state legislator, 9, 13–14; and immigration, 27–28; intellect of, 51–52; and Joint Committee on the Conduct of the War, 96–98; and judicial review, 40–41; and Kansas-Nebraska Act, 24–29, 31, 33; as lawyer, 8–9, 23, 24, 51, 74, 83, 122; Lyceum speech (1838), 11; and Northwest Ordinance (1787), 28, 29, 30; and pardoning power, 122–23, 125; and Peoria, Illinois, speech (1854), 30; and pocket veto, 124; and popular sovereignty, 24–26, 29, 42–44; pragmatism of, 3, 9, 26, 66–67, 71, 83, 97–98, 131–32; and presidential oath, 64; progressivism of, 52; and racism, 16, 33, 46–49, 111–12, 125–27; and Radical Republicans,

91–99, 102–3, 105, 120–26, 131–34; and Reconstruction, 120–26, 132–33; and secession, 60–62; and slavery, 12–16, 17, 26; 56, 99, 124–25, 134; and Southerners, 4, 61–62; and Supreme Court, 42–46; and Thirteenth Amendment, 128–30; and three-fifths clause, 25; and treason, 102, 115–17; and tyranny, 11, 111, 132; and Union, 30, 62–67, 72, 87, 106, 115; and Wade-Davis Bill, 124–26; and West Virginia, 71–72, 83; and Western territories, 33

Louisiana, Reconstruction in, 127–28, 130

Louisiana Purchase (1803), 18–19

Madison, James, 110
Marshall, John, 41
Marshall, Thurgood, 4
martial law, 74
Maryland, 69, 73–74, 79–85
Mason, James, 69
Massachusetts troops: Fifty-Fourth Volunteer Infantry, 97
McClellan, George, 89–91, 94–95, 100, 134
McPherson, James, 2
Merryman, John, 78–79, 85
Mexican War, 21, 52
Missouri, 69, 103
Missouri Compromise. *See* Compromise of 1820
Morrill Land-Grant Colleges Act (1862), 88

National Banking Acts (1862, 1864), 88
natural law, 13, 64. *See also* higher law
Neely, Mark, 2, 75, 79, 85
New Salem, Illinois, 7
New Virginia. *See* West Virginia
Northwest Ordinance (1787), 13, 18, 29, 30

Olustee, Battle of, 97, 114
originalism, 29–30

Paludan, Phillip S., 2
Patterson, James, 97
Peoria, Illinois, 30
Pierpont, Francis H., 70–71
Pocket veto, 124–25
Polk, James K., 52
popular sovereignty, 22–23, 29, 38, 42–49
Port Hudson, Battle of, 114
Potter, David, 43
presidency, 53–56, 64, 79–81, 108
Prize cases (1863), 117–18

Radical Republicans, 86–88, 91–98, 100–103, 105, 120–26, 128–31
Reconstruction, 120–30
Republican Party, 24, 33–35, 41, 51, 65, 83, 86–89, 91–98, 114, 129–30
Revolution, American, 6, 7, 12

Scott, Dred, 35
Scott, Winfield, 57, 75–77
Seward, William, 51, 65
slavery: and Civil War, 56, 99–101; and colonization, 110–12; and compensated emancipation, 110–11; and confiscation acts, 101–2; as contraband, 100–101; and Constitution, 13, 17–18; and Founding Fathers, 13, 25–26; fugitive slaves, 59; and Southerners, 34–35; and Washington DC, 14–15, 59, 108
Spooner, Lysander, 13, 27

spot resolutions, 52
Springfield, Illinois, 22, 28, 40, 60
squatter sovereignty. *See* popular sovereignty
Stanton, Edwin M., 93, 97–98
state suicide theory, 125
Stevens, Thaddeus, 86, 91
Story, Joseph, 8
strict constructionism, 10, 14, 20, 31, 57, 63, 72–73, 80, 88, 89, 108
Sumner, Charles, 86, 119–20, 129
Supreme Court (US), 35, 43–44, 54–55, 79, 82, 84, 102, 113, 116, 117–18, 133–34

Taney, Roger B., 27, 33, 35–42, 49–51, 68–69, 72, 78–85, 87, 102, 119, 123, 134
Tap, Bruce, 95
Taylor, Zachary, 23
Ten Percent Plan, 121–23, 130
treason, 102, 104, 115–17

Virginia, 69–70

Wade, Benjamin, 93, 94–95, 105, 123
Wade-Davis Bill (1864), 123–26, 130
Wadsworth, James S., 127
Washington, DC, 14–15, 60, 108, 120
Washington, George, 6–7, 8, 12
West Point, 94
West Virginia, 70–72, 83, 89–90
Whig Party, 9, 12, 14, 23, 52, 88

Brian R. Dirck is a professor of history at Anderson University in Anderson, Indiana. He specializes in American legal and constitutional history and the American Civil War era. He has written extensively on Abraham Lincoln's politics and legal career.

CONCISE
LINCOLN
LIBRARY

This series of concise books fills a need for short studies of the life, times, and legacy of President Abraham Lincoln. Each book gives readers the opportunity to quickly achieve basic knowledge of a Lincoln-related topic. These books bring fresh perspectives to well-known topics, investigate previously overlooked subjects, and explore in greater depth topics that have not yet received book-length treatment. For a complete list of current and forthcoming titles, see www.conciselincolnlibrary.com.

Other Books in the Concise Lincoln Library

Abraham Lincoln and Horace Greeley
Gregory A. Borchard

Lincoln and the Civil War
Michael Burlingame

Lincoln and the Election of 1860
Michael S. Green

Lincoln and Race
Richard Striner

Abraham and Mary Lincoln
Kenneth J. Winkle